Financial Services for Solicitors

The College of Law
of England and Wales

LIBRARY SERVICES

Related titles from Law Society Publishing:

Marketing Legal Services: Succeeding in the New Legal Marketplace
David Monk and Alastair Moyes

Practice Management Handbook (2nd edn, due 2009)
Edited by Peter Scott

Profitability and Law Firm Management (2nd edn)
Andrew Otterburn

Strategy for Law Firms: After the Legal Services Act 2007 (due 2009)
Nick Jarrett-Kerr and Michael Roch

Titles from Law Society Publishing can be ordered from all good bookshops or direct (telephone 0870 850 1422, email **law.society@prolog.uk.com** or visit our online shop at **www.lawsociety.org.uk/bookshop**).

Financial Services for Solicitors

Law, Practice and Precedents

Edited by Ian Muirhead

The Law Society

ISBN–13: 978–1–85328–754–1

The material in Chapter 17 is reproduced by kind permission of Tru-Est

Published in 2009 by the Law Society
113 Chancery Lane, London WC2A 1PL

Typeset by J&L Composition Ltd, Scarborough, North Yorkshire
Printed by Hobbs the Printers Ltd, Totton, Hants

The paper used for the text pages of this book is FSC certified. FSC (the Forest Stewardship Council) is an international network to promote responsible management of the world's forests.

Contents

About the authors

Editor

Ian Muirhead is a solicitor who started his career with Norton Rose in the City of London and subsequently went into industry as personnel director, company secretary and legal adviser. He reverted to private practice in the 1980s and established a financial planning department as a partner at what is now TWM Solicitors in Surrey. This led to his being asked by other law firms to help them become involved in financial services, and in 1992 he set up SIFA with this objective. SIFA is now the recognised trade body for solicitor financial advisers, and has extended its membership to include accountancy IFAs and financial planners who work with professional practices. Ian was a founder member of the Law Society's Financial Services Working Party and is the author of a number of publications.

Contributors of individual chapters

Lynne Bradey is a solicitor at the Sheffield office of Wrigleys Solicitors LLP. She is a member of STEP, Solicitors for the Elderly and the Law Society's Probate Section. Lynne contributes regularly to *Elderly Client Adviser* magazine and is co-author with David Coldrick of *Coldrick on Personal Injury Trusts*, fourth edition (Ark Group, December 2008). She is a regular speaker and writer on personal injury trusts, vulnerable beneficiary issues, Court of Protection and care fees issues.

Stuart Bushell was a director of the Solicitors Regulation Authority until 2008. As chair of the Law Society's Transition Board he led the Society's response to the Legal Services Act 2007 and the structural changes which resulted, including the creation of the Solicitors Regulation Authority and Legal Complaints Service. Stuart initially joined the Law Society in 1988 to found the Society's Financial Services Monitoring Unit, and left in 1997 to become a director of the Quality Assurance Agency for Higher Education before rejoining the Society in 2002.

Jon Cartwright FCCA ATII TEP is managing partner of Hazlewoods LLP, Cheltenham. As both an accountant and a chartered tax adviser, Jon specialises in advising legal practices and high level tax planning work. He speaks widely on a variety of strategy and tax related matters, as well as holding positions on various national accounting and tax bodies.

Richard Clark BSc (Hons), Diploma PFS (AFPC), IAQ, MAQ, is Financial Planning Manager at Dickinson Dees LLP. Richard specialises in investment and holistic financial planning. He has considerable experience in advising executives in all financial planning matters and regularly provides executive counselling seminars, both locally and nationally. Richard is also a member of Dickinson Dees' specialist SME team providing an all-round service to this sector.

David Coldrick is a partner of Wrigleys Solicitors LLP in charge of the Sheffield office. He is a member of STEP, Solicitors for the Elderly and the Law Society's Probate Section. David contributes regularly to *Elderly Client Adviser* magazine and is co-author of *Coldrick on Personal Injury Trusts*, fourth edition (Ark Group, December 2008). He deals with all areas of private client work, including tax, trusts and estates and has a particular interest and is a well known authority on tax planning for the elderly client and protection of assets of personal injury trusts.

Janet Davies is founder and managing director of national care fees planning group Symponia. Janet is a member of the Faculty of Retirement and Care and holds specialist qualifications in long-term care. She has worked in the care fees planning arena for over 16 years.

Jeremy Davis, MA PhD (Cantab), Dip PFS is managing director of 35 Finance Limited in Cambridge and King's Lynn. Jeremy and his firm work closely with solicitors, particularly Barr Ellison in Cambridge and Kenneth Bush in King's Lynn, who are shareholders in the firm. The specialisations of the firm, in addition to tax planning for expatriates, are in the areas of investments and pensions in wills and probate, conveyancing, matrimonial, personal injury and commercial work.

Clare Douglas is a solicitor in the private client department of Speechly Bircham LLP Solicitors. She advises on a wide range of family law issues, mostly for high net worth clients, including financial disputes, many of which have an international element, and disputes relating to children. She has written for a variety of legal publications and is an Honorary Legal Adviser at the Royal Courts of Justice Advice Bureau.

Noel Farrelly is director of Index Wealth Management, a fee-based invest-ment advisory firm serving the needs of a limited number of wealthy indi-viduals and families. Index was the first and, so far only, national winner of the New Model Adviser award in 2006 for those who have best embraced the 'new model' of fee-based advice and best business practice. Noel is a chartered financial planner and holds the investment management certifi-cate, as well as being a qualified pensions specialist. He is also a fellow and past Board member of the Institute of Financial Planning, and has served as an assessor for the Certified Financial Planner qualification.

James Freeman is a partner at Speechly Bircham LLP Solicitors. James specialises in family law and advises on all issues arising from relation-ship breakdown. He has particular interests in complex financial cases, commonly involving international issues, offshore assets and trusts, and in cohabitation law. He is also experienced in wealth protection matters, including pre- and post-nuptial agreements, many of which also have an international flavour, living together agreements and structuring advice.

Peter Gamson is an audit partner at Grant Thornton UK LLP in London, and head of its national Professional Practices group. He has a broad range of client experience in the professional services sector, working with smaller partnerships and start-up businesses through to large international groups and listed entities. His work includes audit and solicitors' accounts work, strategic advisory, remuneration and reward planning, mergers, IPOs, IFRS conversions and international expansions.

Paul Garwood is head of Personal Financial Planning at Smith & Williamson. Paul is a chartered accountant, a chartered tax adviser and a member of STEP, who specialises in financial planning for high net worth individuals and families. He speaks and writes widely on financial planning issues and is quoted regularly in national newspapers.

Steve Hartley is a corporate solicitor with law firm DWF LLP, based in Leeds and works closely with lead partner John Hartup. Steve specialises in advising regional and national clients in the financial services and general and commercial insurance sectors on a wide range of corporate, commer-cial and insurance related matters, from mergers and acquisitions, finance and structure to day-to-day commercial matters.

Richard Hopkins AFPC, accredited by Resolution, is director and founding principal at Blackstone Moregate, Independent Financial Advisers, London EC1. Richard and his firm work closely with solicitors and accountants to provide professional support to their clients in the areas of inheritance tax planning, investments and pensions.

Adrian Mundell is head of the Court of Protection Team and associate (non-solicitor) at Kester Cunningham John in Thetford, Norfolk. The firm acts as professional deputy for many clients throughout the country, specialising in clients who are either making an injury claim or who have received damages from such claims both from within the firm or on instructions of other firms of solicitors who have clients who may require such support.

Steve Patterson MSFA, Dip PFS, ISO is a certified financial planner. Steve is investment and managing director of CFG Wealth Management, and has an outstanding reputation in designing innovative and robust strategies for investors in both the personal tax and retirement planning fields. He and his wealth management team have provided investment and tax planning services to private investors and their businesses for over 20 years. He is also the founder and managing director of SIPP specialist Intelligent Pensions Ltd, where he manages private pension funds to the value of around £400 million for its clients.

John Porteous FPFS CFP is Head of Private Clients at BDO Stoy Hayward Investment Management. Accredited by Resolution to provide advice on collaborative law assignments, he is both a chartered and certified financial planner. BDO Stoy Hayward Investment Management offers a broad range of financial planning, investment and corporate benefit solutions to private clients, trustees and companies.

Dave Robinson FCCA APFS IMC TEP CFP is a chartered financial planner and director of Albert Goodman Financial Planning Limited in Weston Super Mare, Taunton and Congresbury, which is wholly owned by the partners of Albert Goodman Chartered Accountants. Dave's specialisation is in providing financial planning and investment advice to clients in 'later life', which generally involves a combination of care fees planning, estate planning and inheritance tax mitigation.

Richard Shanks Dip PFS is managing director of Professional Financial Centre (East Midlands) Ltd. His initial investment experience was gained at a national bank, from where he moved to a substantial provincial law firm and specialised in inheritance tax and trust investment planning. The Professional Financial Centre is completely fee based and provides a common resource for local professional firms, majoring on holistic financial planning for individual clients, charities and businesses. Particular importance is attached to explaining to clients the way in which financial advice complements solicitors' and accountants' tax advice.

Foreword

As the professional landscape evolves, solicitors – and especially those in the high street – face challenges in many of the traditional business areas from new competitors.

It is therefore essential that, wherever possible, solicitors widen their field of expertise and examine the opportunities that lie in emerging markets. Being a trusted financial adviser is one such opportunity, and the emergence of so many solicitors recognising the synergy between legal and financial advice represents one of the most exciting developments in the profession.

The unique skills, expertise and experience solicitors possess ideally position them to provide a range of financial advice. This, however, must be coupled with a business-like approach, and that is why my mantra as President of the Law Society of England and Wales is 'the Business of Law'. Today we are not just solicitors, we are all business people.

Packed with detailed information, but also easy to navigate, this handbook provides exactly the sort of advice that solicitors require to meet the challenges and embrace the opportunities of the future.

Paul Marsh
President, Law Society of England and Wales

Preface

The solicitors' profession has conspicuously failed to connect with financial services, despite the obvious synergy between legal and financial work. This can be attributed to a number of factors. First, solicitors' lack of appetite for non-mainstream activities, allied with their institutionalised risk-aversity. Secondly, the absence of an efficient decision-making process within practices, arising in many cases from the anarchy of the partnership structure (solicitors' firms have been described as 'confederations of sole practitioners'). Thirdly, the 'white socks' image of financial advisers, strengthened by a series of 'mis-selling' scandals, has made solicitors wary of involvement.

However, attitudes are beginning to change. Resolution (previously known as the Solicitors' Family Law Association) has established an exam and accreditation scheme for financial advisers wishing to act as financial neutrals in divorce cases. The Institute of Chartered Accountants in England and Wales (ICAEW) has demonstrated that financial services has a legitimate role in the professional service proposition: many acountancy firms have embraced financial planning and the ICAEW has established a financial services faculty to further encourage their efforts.

In addition, there has been a fortuitous coincidence of two major regulatory developments. The Legal Services Act 2007, which is opening up the legal profession to involvement by practitioners from different disciplines, has coincided with the Retail Regulatory Review of the Financial Services Authority, which acknowledges the establishment of a professional cadre among financial advisers, distinguished by fee-based remuneration and advanced qualifications.

The scenario which is evolving is one in which solicitors, accountants and financial advisers are likely to be finding common ground. Research conducted within the solicitors' profession has concluded that if solicitors are to be partnered with other professions, accountants would be the profession of choice; and, as what might be viewed as a half-way house towards such combinations, solicitors are expressing significant interest in establishing financial services joint ventures with accountants.

This handbook is designed to assist solicitors to identify and take advantage of the business opportunities arising out of financial services work. It considers the regulatory, legal, commercial and marketing issues, and goes on to discuss some of the main areas in which financial advice impacts on solicitors' mainstream work.

The law is stated as at 5 December 2008.

Ian Muirhead
Managing Director, SIFA
December 2008

Abbreviations

Accounts Rules	Solicitors' Accounts Rules 1998
ABS	alternative business structure
AIM	alternative investment market
AJD	*impuesto sobre actos juridicos documentados* (stamp duty in Spain)
APF	authorised professional firm
APR	agricultural property relief
AR	appointed representative
ASP	alternatively secured pension
ATP	authorised third party
BPR	business property relief
CGT	capital gains tax
CLT	chargeable lifetime transfer
CRAG	*Charging for Residential Accommodation Guide*
CSOP	company share option plan
DGT	discounted gift trust
DPB	designated professional body
EBIT	earnings before interest and tax
EMI	enterprise management incentive
EPA	enduring power of attorney
EPF	exempt professional firm
FSA	Financial Services Authority
FSMA 2000	Financial Services and Markets Act 2000
GPP	group personal pension
HMRC	Her Majesty's Revenue and Customs
IFA	independent financial adviser
IHT	inheritance tax
IIP	interest in possession
IP	*impuesto sobre el patrimonio* (wealth tax in Spain)
IRPF	*impuesto sobre la renta de las personas fisicas* (income tax in Spain)
ISD	*impuesto de sucesiones y donaciones* (succession tax in Spain)
IT	income tax
ITP	*impuesto sobre transmisiones patrimoniales* (tax payable on the transfer of value between private individuals)

JV	joint venture
LAP	life assurance policy
LDP	legal disciplinary practice
LLP	limited liability partnership
LPA	lasting power of attorney
LSB	Legal Services Board
LTC	Long Term Care
MDP	multi-disciplinary practice
NMRA	non-mainstream regulated activity
OEIC	open-ended investment company
OPG	Office of the Public Guardian
PAYE	Pay As You Earn
PCT	primary care trust
PET	potentially exempt transfer
PIF	personal investment firm
PLA	purchased life annuity
PHI	permanent health insurance
PMI	private medical insurance
PNA	pre-nuptial agreement
POAT	pre-owned asset tax
PWC	PricewaterhouseCoopers
QROPS	qualifying recognised overseas pension scheme
RAT	rate applicable to trusts
REL	registered European lawyer
RNCC	Registered Nursing Care Contribution
Scope Rules	Solicitors' Financial Services (Scope) Rules 2001
SAYE	Save As You Earn
SCI	*société civile immobilière*
SHIP	Safe Home Income Plans
SICAV	*société d'investissement à capital variable* (open-ended collective investment scheme common in Western Europe)
SIP	share incentive plan
SIPP	self-invested personal pension
SRA	Solicitors Regulation Authority
SSAS	small self-administered scheme
UCIT	undertakings for collective investment in transferable securities
USP	unsecured pension

1

Regulation and structures for financial services

Financial services regulation and the professions

Ian Muirhead

The Financial Services and Markets Act 2000

The Financial Services and Markets Act 2000 (FSMA 2000) created a new regulatory framework for the UK and a single financial services regulator – the Financial Services Authority (FSA). All firms wishing to undertake regulated activity, such as providing investment or mortgage advice, must apply to the FSA for authorisation, and this will be granted subject to completion of a lengthy and detailed application designed to reassure the FSA that the firm has a viable business plan, that it has adequate financial resources and that it has on its staff individuals who are able to demonstrate, by reference to their qualifications and their fitness and propriety, that they should be accredited as 'approved persons'.

Professional firms may apply for FSA authorisation and, if granted, they will be subject to dual regulation – by their professional body and by the FSA. Such firms are known as 'authorised professional firms' (APFs) and they enjoy two advantages over other FSA-authorised advisory firms (which are known as 'personal investment firms' (PIFs)):

- Solicitor firms (but not accountancy firms) which are FSA-authorised are exempt from the Financial Services Compensation Scheme levy, on the basis that their professional scheme provides broadly equivalent benefits.
- They are exempt from the requirements of the EU Capital Requirements Directive. This imposes risk-based capital adequacy criteria and could become onerous if, as has been mooted, the requirement were to be calculated not as a fixed sum but as an expenditure-based requirement equal to three months' overheads.

In order to qualify for APF status, firms' FSA-regulated activities must represent less than 50 per cent of their total income and must not be promoted in such a way as to suggest to clients that the regulated business which they conduct is other than a complement to their professional work.

Certain activities fall outside the ambit of FSMA 2000 and are excluded from the scope of the Act:

- Activity carried out by a trustee or personal representative, provided that he does not hold himself out as providing a regulated service and does not receive additional remuneration for such service.
- Activities carried on in the course of a profession, which may reasonably be regarded as a necessary part of other services provided by the professional.
- Activities carried on in connection with the acquisition or disposal of shares in a body corporate consisting of or including 50 per cent or more of the voting shares.

Other activities are regarded as being incidental to professional work, as opposed to being a necessary part of such work, and provision has been made for such activities to be 'exempted' from FSMA 2000 rather than being 'excluded' from it. In order to qualify for exemption, activities must comply with the conditions laid down by FSMA 2000, s.327, of which the most important are:

- that the professional must not receive from a person other than his client any pecuniary reward or other advantage for which he does not account to his client;
- that the activities must be incidental to the provision of professional services and must arise out of or be complementary to those services.

The FSA's *Professional Firms Handbook* at 5.2.1 classifies such activities as 'non-mainstream regulated activities' (NMRAs) and provides that they should be subject to regulation by the professional bodies, which are referred to in the Act as 'designated professional bodies' (DPBs). Firms which enjoy the benefit of this exemption are known as 'exempt professional firms' (EPFs) and are listed as such on the FSA website at **www.fsa.gov.uk**. Law firms in England and Wales which wish to confine themselves to exempt regulated activity are automatically permitted to avail themselves of the exemption for DPB firms, and need make no application to the Law Society for permission. However, they are required to submit to the Society annual returns detailing the members of the firm who are likely to be involved in such business. In Scotland, firms are required to register with the Law Society and pay the required fee in order to qualify for EPF status.

The rules made by the Law Society in its capacity as a DPB (a function which has now been passed to the Solicitors Regulation Authority (SRA)) are the Solicitors' Financial Services (Scope) Rules 2001 (which set out the scope of the activities which may be undertaken by firms under the Part

XX exemption) and the Solicitors' Financial Services (Conduct of Business) Rules 2001 (which relate to the conduct of regulated activities).

The rules administered by the SRA enable it to regulate the exempt activities of those of its members which are authorised by the FSA for mainstream investment business, but the rules adopted by the other main DPBs (the ICAEW and the Scottish Law Society, in particular) do not give them this power. Consequently, solicitors and fee-earners in English and Welsh law firms who are not FSA-authorised can arrange general insurance and provide discretionary investment management services under the auspices of the SRA, whereas other APFs must undertake such activities under direct FSA regulation.

All APFs are permitted to conduct discretionary portfolio management and to hold client money and assets in connection with their legal services without the need for risk-based capital adequacy, subject only to the Financial Services (Conduct of Business) Rules 2001. However, if they were, for example, to offer custody services in connection with an FSA-regulated activity, they would become subject to the FSA's custody rules.

It should be noted that within an APF, only those members of the firm who have been recognised for FSA purposes as approved persons may conduct mainstream regulated activities.

The Solicitors' Financial Services (Scope) Rules 2001

The Solicitors' Financial Services (Scope) Rules 2001 (the Scope Rules) (which have been amended in some minor respects by the Solicitors' Financial Services (Scope) Amendment Rules 2009) dovetail with the provisions of Part XX of FSMA 2000 and require that firms which are not authorised by FSA must ensure when carrying on any exempt regulated activities that:

- the activities arise out of, or are complementary to, the provision of a professional service other than a regulated activity;
- the manner of the provision of the service is incidental to the provision of those professional services;
- the firm accounts to its clients for any pecuniary or other advantage which it receives from any third party (including any authorised third party with or through whom the professional may be working);
- the activities are not specifically proscribed;
- the firm does not hold itself out as carrying on a regulated activity other than as permitted by the Scope Rules.

The Scope Rules go on to prohibit firms operating within the Part XX exemption from undertaking certain specific activities. These may be summarised as follows:

- Firms must not recommend or make arrangements for clients to buy a packaged investment product except where the transaction takes the form of an assignment; or the activity relates to discretionary portfolio management services carried out by an authorised third party; or the transaction is execution-only.
- Firms must not recommend that clients buy or dispose of any rights or interests in a personal pension scheme except on an execution-only basis, provided in the latter case that the transaction does not involve transfers or opt-outs from an occupational pension scheme.
- Firms must not recommend that clients subscribe for securities or contractually based investments (this does not apply to clients who are not individuals).
- Firms must not provide discretionary portfolio management services except when the firm is, or members of the firm are, acting as trustee, personal representative, donee of a power of attorney or deputy appointed by the Court of Protection, and transactions are undertaken by or in accordance with the advice of an FSA-authorised person.
- Firms must not act as sponsors to issues of securities on the London Stock Exchange or the Alternative Investment Market.
- Firms which are not listed on the FSA Register as exempt professional firms must not conduct general insurance business.
- Firms must not recommend regulated mortgage contracts or equity release schemes, but may endorse recommendations made by authorised persons.

Conducting a referral relationship with an 'authorised third party' (ATP – see Chapter 3) would clearly fall within the Part XX exemption; and the following types of activity would be permitted to authorised firms on the basis that they qualify as being incidental to solicitors' professional services:

- actioning execution-only instructions;
- advising on the disposal or assignment of investments (other than personal pension schemes);
- advising on the tax considerations affecting the quantum of contributions to pensions, ISAs and other tax-advantaged investments;
- providing custody services in conjunction with the provision of legal services;
- as a trustee, making recommendations to a fellow trustee or a beneficiary in connection with dealings by or in a trust;

- giving 'negative clearance' (i.e. assenting to the recommendation of an ATP, or to the client's own decision).

In summary, the activities which may be undertaken by EPFs fall under two main heads:

- Financial services activities which are incidental to the work of professional firms and arise out of or are complementary to the provision of a professional service which is not FSA-regulated. Many APFs have permission to conduct the activity of 'managing investments' (typically in the context of trust work) on a non-mainstream basis.
- Arrangements made with or through an ATP, such as a stockbroker or an external independent financial adviser (IFA), provided that the firm accounts to the client for any pecuniary or other advantage which it receives from such third party.

The Solicitors' Financial Services (Conduct of Business) Rules 2001

These rules deal with compliance and record-keeping for exempt regulated activities. In relation to solicitors' business referrals to IFAs, they impose a number of undemanding requirements, which correspond broadly with those applicable to what was termed 'non-discrete investment business' under the Law Society's old Solicitors' Investment Business Rules. The main requirements are as follows:

- Status disclosure, involving the provision of the following information:

  - name and address of the firm;
  - a statement that it is not authorised by the FSA;
  - a statement of the nature of the regulated activities carried on by the firm and the fact of their being limited in scope;
  - a statement that the firm is regulated by the SRA;
  - a statement that complaints and redress procedures are available through the SRA and the Legal Complaints Service.

- Firms which are involved in general insurance business must make the following statement to their clients, in writing:

  We are not authorised by the Financial Services Authority. However, we are included on the register maintained by the Financial Services Authority so that we can carry on insurance mediation activity, which is broadly the advising on, selling and administration of insurance contracts. This part of our business, including arrangements for complaints and redress if something goes wrong, is regulated by the Solicitors Regulation Authority. The register can be accessed via the Financial Services Authority website at **www.fsa.gov.uk/register**.

- A record of instructions, showing the name of the client, the terms of the instructions, the date when they were given and the name of the person instructed. This can take the form of a file note, an attendance note or a letter.
- A record of any commissions received, showing the amount and how the firm accounted to the client. This could take the form of a letter or a bill. The term 'commissions' encompasses 'any pecuniary reward or other advantage'.
- Where a firm provides custody services it must operate appropriate systems and maintain appropriate records. Where responsibility for custody is passed to a third party it must obtain a receipt for the property involved, and where the third party services were arranged on the instructions of the client, the client's instructions must be obtained in writing.
- Where the firm arranges an execution-only transaction, it must send the client written confirmation that the client has not sought and was not given any advice by the firm, or that having been advised against the transaction, the client nevertheless persisted with the instruction.
- All records maintained in accordance with these rules must be kept for at least six years.

The Solicitors' Code of Conduct 2007

The Solicitors' Code of Conduct 2007 (the Code), which has been revised with effect from March 2009 by the Solicitors' Code of Conduct (LDPs and Firm Based Regulation) Amendment Rules 2009, complements the Scope Rules and the Conduct of Business Rules, and rule 19 of the Code lays down the wider principles governing solicitors' involvement in financial services.

Insofar as concerns regulated financial services activity, rule 19 sets out the requirements for ensuring that solicitors' independence is preserved by prohibiting solicitors from:

- being an appointed representative;
- having any arrangement with other persons under which they could be constrained to recommend to clients or effect for them (or refrain from so doing) transactions in some investments but not others, with some persons but not others, or through the agency of some persons but not others;
- having any arrangement with other persons under which they could be constrained to introduce or refer clients or other persons with whom they deal to some persons but not others;

- having any active involvement in a solicitors' separate business which is an appointed representative, unless it is the appointed representative of an independent financial adviser.

Rule 19 stresses that 'independence is a core duty', but it provides specifically that this would not prevent a solicitor from regularly introducing clients to a particular broker (which term would include other types of financial intermediary), provided that there was no arrangement which could constrain the solicitor to using only that broker.

However, the principle of independence does not extend to general insurance business. Subrule 9.03 of the Code states:

(1) If you recommend that a client use a particular firm, agency or business, you must do so in good faith, judging what is in the client's best interests.

(2) You must not enter into any agreement or association which would restrict your freedom to recommend any particular firm, agency or business.

(3) (2) above does not apply to arrangements in connection with any of the following types of contracts:

    (a) regulated mortgage contracts;
    (b) general insurance contracts; or
    (c) pure protection contracts.

(4) The terms 'regulated mortgage contracts', 'general insurance contracts' and 'pure protection contracts' in (3) above have the meanings given in 19.01(4).

(5) Where you refer a client to a firm, agency or business that can only offer products from one source, you must notify the client in writing of this limitation.

Solicitors' separate businesses

A solicitor's separate business is defined in rule 21 of the Code as 'a business which is not regulated by the Solicitors Regulation Authority but which provides "solicitor-like" services', i.e. services which could be carried out as part of a legal practice but are conducted other than under the regulation of the SRA. The purpose of rule 21 (which was amended with effect from March 2009 to take account of legal disciplinary practices (LDPs) and firm-based regulation) is to ensure that members of the public are not confused or misled into believing that a business carried on by a solicitor or a registered European lawyer (REL) is regulated by the SRA when it is not.

Rule 21.05 provides for the following safeguards:

- The separate business must not be held out or described in such a way as to suggest that it carries on a practice regulated by the SRA, or that any lawyer connected with a solicitors' firm is providing services through the separate business as a practising lawyer regulated by the SRA.

- All paperwork, documents, records or files relating to the separate business and its customers must be kept separate from those of any firm or in-house practice, even where a customer of the separate business is also a client of the firm or in-house practice.
- The client account used for any firm or in-house practice must not be used to hold money for the separate business, or for customers of the separate business in their capacity as such.
- If the separate business shares premises, office accommodation or reception staff with any firm or in-house practice, the areas used by the firm or in-house practice must be clearly differentiated from the areas used by the separate business; and all clients of the separate business must be informed that it is not regulated by the SRA and that the statutory protections attaching to clients of a lawyer regulated by the SRA are not available to them as customers of that business.
- If solicitors refer clients to the separate business, the clients must first be informed of the solicitors' interest in the separate business, that the separate business is not regulated by the SRA, and that the statutory protections attaching to clients of a lawyer regulated by the SRA are not available to clients of the separate business.

The Law Society of Scotland has no rules or formal guidance corresponding to those governing solicitors' separate businesses in England. It trusts its members to use their common sense to ensure that solicitor/client confidentiality is maintained. Where premises are shared, different nameplates must appear at the front door; and it must be made clear by way of a business card that the separate business is not part of the solicitor's firm.

The separate business rule will be clearly be subject to modification when the rules governing alternative business structures (ABSs) are created (see Chapter 7).

2

The Legal Services Act 2007

Stuart Bushell

Background to the Act

Historically there have been tight restrictions on the types of business through which legal services could be provided. Lawyers have been prevented from entering into partnerships with other legal professionals and with non-lawyers, and prevented also from offering stakes in the ownership of their firms to non-solicitors.

This state of affairs was regarded by consumer groups and the government as anti-competitive, and in March 2001 the Office of Fair Trading produced a report which concluded that a number of the professional rules governing the practice of law were unduly restrictive. The government seized on this as providing the opportunity to achieve its wider objective of benefiting consumers by giving them greater choice, better service, reduced prices and improved access to justice. It therefore appointed Sir David Clementi to investigate, and in 2005 he produced a 'Review of the Regulatory Framework for Legal Services in England and Wales'.

The Clementi Review recommended that the rules should be relaxed to permit the creation of legal disciplinary practices (LDPs), i.e. combinations of different types of lawyer, including solicitors, barristers, licensed conveyancers, notaries public, legal executives and patent and trade mark agents. The government accepted this proposal but went further by stating its preference for a move towards the full multi-disciplinary practice (MDP) which had originally been envisaged but which Clementi had considered 'a bridge too far'.

The Legal Services Act 2007, which resulted from the Clementi Review, enables both LDPs and MDPs (now re-named alternative business structures (ABSs)) in England and Wales (the Scottish Parliament is considering its own version). However, different timescales are attached to the two variants. LDPs have been permitted since March 2009 and are regulated in England and Wales by the Solicitors Regulation Authority (SRA), but it will take until 2011 or 2012 until the arrival of ABSs, which will be able to conduct both legal and non-legal work and will potentially involve multiple regulators, become a reality.

The scope provided by the ABS model for law firms to be controlled by non-lawyers opens the door to the provision of legal services by commercial organisations ('Tesco Law') and the possibility of law firms converting to public limited company status and possibly going on to seek a Stock Exchange quotation.

The structure of the Law Society is also undergoing major change. Addressing concerns about the apparent conflict of interest arising out of the fact that the Law Society was historically both a regulator and a representative body for solicitors, the regulatory function has now been delegated to the SRA. The Act also addresses a long-standing concern that complaints handling should be separated from both the regulatory and representative activities of legal professional bodies, and has created a new Office for Legal Complaints, with responsibility for handling complaints against the various types of lawyer.

The Law Society of England and Wales has been given new powers by the Act, many of which are to be used by the SRA, whose own rules, including the Solicitors' Code of Conduct 2007 (the Code), have also been extensively amended as a result of the Act.

The SRA has taken the opportunity to adopt 'firm-based regulation', on similar lines to the Financial Services Authority (FSA), extending its regulatory powers to include firms as well as individuals. The Recognised Bodies Regulations 2009 which have been created by the SRA will apply to firms, their managers, their owners and their employees. Firms will be subject to the SRA disciplinary sanctions and those of the Solicitors Disciplinary Tribunal.

Firm-based regulation for solicitors and others regulated by the SRA commenced in March 2009, when all existing firms of solicitors were 'passported' into the new regime and thus became 'recognised bodies'. New practices and LDPs have been required to apply for recognition by the SRA or another front-line regulator and to submit to investigation of their past regulatory record and their business experience. However, participation in LDPs is not based on any specific professional qualification or discipline.

Legal disciplinary practices

The legislation permits greater flexibility in the composition of an LDP than was envisaged by Clementi, in that this model can now include not only different combinations of lawyers but also up to 25 per cent non-lawyers. However, the services provided must essentially be legal services, regulated by the SRA or another approved legal regulator.

Technically, under the Legal Services Act 2007, LDPs are simply a form of ABS. Non-lawyers are required to apply for approval by the SRA to participate, but those interested in becoming external owners will have to wait until the advent of ABSs in 2011 or 2012. Also, LDPs must be managed by lawyers, of whatever type; the term 'manager' is defined by the Act as a partner in a partnership, director of a company or member of a limited liability partnership (LLP). This restriction is intended to prevent LDPs from becoming full multi-disciplinary ABSs before the legislation permits – a situation on which the SRA has made it clear that it intends to take a hard line.

Although non-lawyer participants in an LDP must be managers, no such requirement applies to lawyers. In relation to an incorporated practice, this means that a non-lawyer can only be a shareholder if he or she is also a director. Non-lawyer applicants to the SRA (including accountants) are not required to undertake any specific training but do need to pay for a Criminal Records Bureau check. Once approved, non-lawyers do not need to renew their approval, but the SRA has power to remove it for a variety of reasons; and the approval will automatically lapse after two years from the point at which the non-lawyer ceases to be a manager of an LDP.

There is a base of evidence which suggests that, in numerical terms, there may be a significant take-up of LDPs. However, the likelihood is that most of the participants are likely to be barristers and managers already involved in law firms as employees, for example CEOs, marketing managers and finance managers. Providers of non-legal professional services, such as financial advisers, are unlikely to regard a minority equity participation in a solicitors' practice as an attractive option. An ABS is likely to be more attractive and practical, though the joint venture options described in Chapter 4 may prove to be the most durable model for independent financial advisers (IFAs) even after the introduction of ABSs in 2011 or 2012.

Compared with LDPs, relatively little information is available as to how ABSs will be allowed to operate. However, it is expected that approved regulators such as the SRA will become licensing authorities for ABSs, subject to approval by the Legal Services Board and the Secretary of State, and that firms wishing to form ABSs will have to apply to the SRA or other approved regulator for a licence. Any firm providing 'regulated legal services' and in which a non-lawyer has an interest, or are able to exercise control, will also require such a licence.

The Act invites the possibility that practitioners will be able to choose between alternative regulators, and that competition will therefore ensue between regulators – the concept known as 'regulatory arbitrage'. In this situation there is clearly a need for a super-regulator, charged with responsibility for recognising front-line regulators and monitoring their activities. Hence the creation by the Act of the Legal Services Board (LSB).

The LSB will license the various potential regulators of LDPs, ABSs and other types of provider of legal services, all of whom will need to apply for approval. The SRA has declared its intention to become licensed and is likely to be the predominant regulator, but other eligible regulators are also likely to seek approval. Both the Council for Licensed Conveyancers and the Institute of Legal Executives may seek to extend their range of permitted members' activities, though it is still difficult to see either as a significant regulatory competitor to the SRA for ABSs. Non-lawyers involved in ABSs will need to check the extent of the permissions to conduct legal services which can be granted by alternative regulators. Recognition granted by the Council for Licensed Conveyancers, for example, would be confined to the provision of conveyancing services.

SRA guidance on arrangements for LDPs emphasises the need to ensure that the solicitors' core duty of independence is not compromised (subrule 1.03 of the Code). There are several examples of situations which might put a firm's independence at risk, for instance:

- finance arrangements or loans with particular strings attached;
- financial arrangements that suggest dependency upon an outside body which could, at that firm's discretion, effectively put the firm of solicitors out of business;
- relationships with third parties that suggest the firm of solicitors is a subsidiary of a third party, rather than independent;
- fee sharing arrangements that go beyond subrule 8.02 of the Code.

It is clear that over-reliance on a single source of work or too close a financial relationship with a third party could be regarded as compromising independence. The SRA guidance makes it plain that before making any arrangement which may conflict with the core duties, a firm of solicitors should identify the risks involved and consider what safeguards could be put in place to eliminate them. This risk analysis must be documented and the safeguards identified.

Alternative business structures

According to the Legal Services Act 2007, s.72(3), a person will be regarded as having an interest in an ABS if he or she holds shares in it or is entitled to exercise, or control the exercise of, voting rights in the body. Section 72 also seeks to cover an 'indirect interest' in a body. The issue of indirect interests is complex and has resulted in the past in much difficulty for other regulators. It is reasonable to expect considerable debate on this subject and further changes to regulators' rules.

Potential ABS firms will need to comply with a number of safeguards in order to be licensed:

- Non-lawyers who own more than 10 per cent of an ABS will be subject to a 'fitness to own' test. There are two elements to this. First, whether the ownership is compatible with the statutory regulatory objectives; and secondly, whether they are fit and proper to own the interest. Each application is to be considered on its own merits.

- Licensing regulators are subject to a statutory duty to avoid conflicts of interest as far as possible. This operates on two levels – that of individuals' internal conflicts as well as conflicts between licensing authorities and other regulators. The FSA is one of the regulators which the Ministry of Justice had in mind in drafting this restriction but it is far from clear as to how, in practice, it is expected that such conflicts might be resolved.
- Firms will need to appoint a Head of Legal Practice and a Head of Finance and Administration for the purposes of accounting to their regulator.
- In particular circumstances, investors can be divested of their shares.
- There are some exemptions and waivers of certain licensing requirements. Some 'low risk' bodies with less than 10 per cent non-lawyer ownership or management will be entitled to take advantage of this lighter regulation, as will not-for-profit bodies.
- After some prolonged debate, it has been decided that clients of ABSs will have the same rights to legal professional privilege as clients of typical law firms, provided that communications with a licensed body are carried out by or through a lawyer.

Guidance issued by the SRA makes clear that firms must not enter into a binding agreement to set up an ABS before rules are introduced which permit these to exist. Non-binding agreements are possible, but even so solicitors should be careful on several points:

- not to compromise their independence;
- not to sell any interest in a firm;
- not to put any future business partner in control of decisions about the business;
- to make certain that any future business partner is not allowed to affect the way in which the firm of solicitors acts for clients;
- not to put any outsider in *de facto* control of partners', members' or directors' meetings.

The 'recognised body' regime

The advent of the recognised body regime has caused the SRA to change a number of key sets of rules:

- Solicitors' Code of Conduct 2007;
- Solicitors' Accounts Rules 1998;

- Solicitors' Indemnity Insurance Rules 2008;
- Solicitors' Compensation Fund Rules 1995;
- Solicitors' Financial Services (Scope) Rules 2001.

All of these changed in March 2009. The Solicitors' Financial Services (Scope) Rules 2001 (discussed in Chapter 1) have been amended in order to deal with the language of firm-based regulation and LDPs, but none of the amendments are substantive amendments; and the Financial Services (Conduct of Business) Rules 2001, also discussed in Chapter 1, are unchanged.

The Solicitors' Code of Conduct 2007 is substantially amended, but the changes do not affect financial services work. Rule 21, on solicitors' separate businesses, is amended to ensure that clients enjoy the statutory protections in relation to certain mainstream legal services and in relation to the whole of any matter involving mainstream legal services work. Rule 19, on financial services and the need for advice to be independent (except in relation to general insurance business), is unaffected by the changes.

The Solicitors' Accounts Rules 1998 (Accounts Rules) are amended to deal with the effect of the Legal Services Act 2007 and now cover LDPs and apply to the individual managers and employees of those practices. All managers are permitted to authorise client account withdrawals but must have an appropriate understanding of the Accounts Rules. The revised Accounts Rules also change the nature of accountants' reports and impose a mandatory whistle-blowing duty on reporting accountants.

The revised Accounts Rules also have the important effect of abolishing the concept of the 'controlled trust', i.e. a trust where a solicitor is the sole trustee or is a co-trustee with a partner or employee of the same firm. All money held by a practice will either be client money or office money. This means that the same interest provisions apply to all client money, including money previously described as 'controlled trust money'.

This change does not affect the common law principle affecting trusts whose only trustees are members of the same firm, namely that trustees must not make a secret profit from their position and that they should not, therefore, refer trust investment work to an organisation in which they have a financial interest, such as a joint venture with an IFA. It has been suggested that financial services work for such trusts should not be handled even by an in-house financial services department, but the preferred view seems to be that there would be no objection to this provided that the necessary work was remunerated by fee rather than commission. Arguably, the simplest way of avoiding the issue altogether would be to appoint an external trustee, so that the profit derived would no longer fall to be regarded as 'secret'.

The Legal Services Act 2007 and the SRA's Recognised Bodies Regulations restrict the activities which may be conducted via a recognised body to 'solicitor services' (see also the comments in relation to solicitors' separate businesses in Chapter 1). This term is not adequately defined anywhere but is intended to mean those services which solicitors or other lawyers can claim to be a legitimate part of their business. It is not the same concept as the 'reserved' activities which only solicitors are permitted to perform, and which centre mainly around litigation.

The naming of a recognised body is covered by reg.11 of the Recognised Bodies Regulations 2009. An LLP will be recognised under its corporate name and a partnership must elect to have a name under which it will be recognised. The SRA has used the new rules as a vehicle to expand the type and quantity of information it requires from firms for inclusion on the public register which it maintains. This now includes all practising styles and addresses, whether a body is a partnership, company or LLP, and it identifies non-lawyers by name.

The SRA's criteria for recognising an LDP

The Recognised Bodies Regulations 2009 contain the details required for an application to become a recognised body. The process as it applies to new firms containing non-lawyers is set out below; and existing firms are passported into the scheme. Applications must include:

- a correctly completed application form;
- a due fee and compensation fund payment;
- such additional information, documents and references as the SRA specifies in advance;
- any additional information and documentation which the SRA reasonably requires.

Regulation 2 sets out basic pre-conditions for the SRA to grant recognition, such as:

- Solicitors' Code of Conduct 2007 requirements on formation, composition, structure, registered office and practising addresses;
- indemnity insurance provisions;
- Solicitors' Code of Conduct 2007 requirements on managers being 'qualified to supervise'.

There is, however, an extensive and wide-ranging set of criteria governing the SRA's discretion to refuse recognition. Among the most significant of these are:

- The SRA is not satisfied that a manager is suitable, taking into account that person's history, character, conduct or associations.
- The SRA is not satisfied that the managers, as a group, can operate or control the business.

- Any event which calls into question a manager's honesty, integrity or respect for law.
- Any failure or refusal to disclose, or attempt to conceal, any such event.
- Any other reason which makes the SRA reasonably consider that it would be against the public interest to grant recognition.

These criteria are stringent and somewhat subjective. Much will rest upon the manner in which the SRA chooses to interpret and apply its discretion.

The eligibility and suitability criteria for non-lawyers are contained in reg.3. The application must be made the recognised body in question. It cannot be made by a non-lawyer on a general basis. The application is expected to demonstrate the following:

- that the individual meets the criteria;
- the firm's co-operation and its assistance to ensure the individual's co-operation, in providing all the information and documentation required, on the application form and otherwise.

As for recognised bodies, above, the detailed criteria are set out in the application form itself. However, the 'unsuitability' factors are listed in the Regulations – the recognised body, non-lawyer or another firm in which the non-lawyer has been a manager or employee:

- has been disciplined or ordered to pay costs by the Solicitors Disciplinary Tribunal;
- has been struck off or suspended by the court;
- has been disciplined, intervened in by the SRA or notified that its response to an SRA request for explanation is unsatisfactory;
- has been disciplined or refused registration or authorisation by another professional, regulatory or disciplinary authority;
- has been committed to prison or charged with any indictable offence;
- has been disqualified as a company director or removed as the trustee of a charity;
- has been declared insolvent or been subject to an outstanding money judgment;
- lacks capacity under the Mental Capacity Act 2005;
- has been involved in conduct which calls into question honesty, integrity or respect for the law;
- fails or refuses to disclose, or tries to hide any of the issues set out above.

This is a comprehensive list and the SRA also has wide powers to impose conditions upon recognition and to request further information from the body or the individual. Recognition renewal is an annual process, effective from 31 October each year.

3

Client referrals to authorised third parties

Ian Muirhead

Documentation

It will usually be appropriate for law firms which refer clients to an independent financial adviser (IFA) to provide Terms of Business for financial services separately from the firm's client care letter for legal business. The Financial Services Authority (FSA) prescribes the content of the Terms for the firms which it regulates and the Solicitors Regulation Authority (SRA), in the Solicitors' Financial Services (Conduct of Business) Rules 2001 (see Chapter 1), prescribes the less comprehensive contents of Terms for firms which refer clients to an authorised third party (ATP). An example of the latter is shown as Precedent B, and this may suitably be supported by a client marketing leaflet such as that shown as Precedent C. A form of letter introducing an ATP IFA to a client is shown as Precedent D.

It is good practice, though not mandatory, for firms which appoint an ATP also to have in place a formal document evidencing the terms of the relationship, and an example of such a document is shown as Precedent A.

The Conduct of Business Rules require a formal record of instructions given to ATPs, and this also makes good business sense. In the same way as a medical GP would instruct a specialist, or a financial adviser might instruct a discretionary portfolio manager, the solicitor needs to be seen to be co-ordinating advice on behalf of the client if he or she is to take advantage of the financial advice process to maintain ongoing contact with the client. In this context the solicitor might at the same time be providing money laundering proof of identity to the IFA, so as to avoid having to put the client through this formality for a second time. An example of a referral instruction is shown as Precedent H.

One of the incidental benefits of a formal instruction procedure is that it should assist in controlling the quality of referrals. Too many solicitors have in the past referred clients to IFAs without giving proper consideration to whether they were the types of client with whom the IFA might be able to build a successful relationship of ongoing benefit to both solicitor and IFA. The professional IFA proposition is not for everyone and IFAs have become much more discriminating in the clients they accept. So in the interests of both solicitor and IFA it is important that only clients whose needs and circumstances fit the IFA's business model should be referred.

Commissions

A record must be maintained of commissions received from ATPs. Subrule 2.06 of the Solictors' Code of Conduct 2007 reads:

> If you are a principal in a firm you must ensure that your firm pays to your client commission received over £20 unless the client, having been told the amount, or if the precise amount is not known, an approximate amount or how the amount is to be calculated, has agreed that your firm may keep it.

Expanding on this principle, the guidance attaching to rule 2.06 reads:

> 57. Commission received may be retained only if the conditions within 2.06 are complied with and the arrangement is in your client's best interests – either:
>
> (a) it is used to offset a bill of costs; or
> (b) you must be able to justify its retention – for example, the commission is retained in lieu of costs which you could have billed for work done in placing the business, but were not so billed.

Commission is defined in the guidance:

> 53. A commission:
>
> (a) is a financial benefit you receive by reason of and in the course of the relationship of solicitor and client; and
> (b) arises in the context that you have put a third party and the client in touch with one another . . .
>
> 54. Examples of what amounts to a commission include payments received from a stockbroker on the purchase of stocks and shares, from an insurance company or an intermediary on the purchase or renewal of an insurance policy, and from a bank or building society on the opening of a bank account . . .

Clients must give their 'informed consent' to solicitors retaining commission, which they can only do if the solicitor has provided details of the amount and made clear that the client can withhold his or her consent and that if they do so the commission will belong to the client when it is received by the solicitor.

The SRA is taking a sterner line than its predecessor the Law Society to the enforcement of these provisions, and is demanding that firms which retain commission should demonstrate that it was in their clients' best interests that they should have done so. It also insists that the consent should be obtained by the solicitor and not by the IFA on the solicitor's behalf. Blanket consents are not acceptable, and a central record must be kept of each individual form of consent.

It would in theory be possible for solicitors to construct an audit trail to demonstrate their justification for retaining commissions, detailing the extent to which information had been shared, joint meetings conducted and copy correspondence reviewed. However, such procedures tend to be contrived, and increasingly solicitors are preferring to avoid the awkwardness of accounting to their clients, and are declining to accept commission payments. This practice has become more common with the increased adoption of fee-based remuneration by financial advisers, which effectively precludes sharing. Relationships with financial advisers are therefore more likely now to be based on solicitors wishing to provide a more comprehensive service to their clients and to ensure that the clients receive advice of a quality which will reflect well on the solicitors as referrers. The closer the rapport between the firms, the greater also will be the opportunity for reciprocal business referrals.

Sharing offices with IFAs

Some firms have entered into arrangements with ATP IFAs whereby nominated advisers attend firms' offices on a regular basis to hold 'surgeries' and in some cases this has extended to the provision of a permanent *pied à terre* for the IFA in the solicitors' office. The latter type of arrangement can give rise to serious concerns on the part of the SRA, as shown by a decision of the Solicitors Disciplinary Tribunal in late 2008 in which a breach of client confidentiality was held to have occurred. All the partners in a firm were reprimanded and one partner fined for failure to account properly for commissions received. The underlying concern of the SRA in relation to such arrangements is that clients should not be led to assume that external financial advisers are part of the law firm and that consequently the statutory protections available to solicitors' clients apply to the financial advice provided.

Identifying professional IFAs

Too many firms leave it to the discretion of individual partners and fee-earners as to which IFAs to favour with referrals. In consequence, inappropriate or ineffective relationships are sometimes established and control is lost over the quality of financial advice given to clients. Some firms establish formal firm-wide relations with a particular firm of IFAs and others, perhaps in the hope of avoiding responsibility for recommendations the suitability of which might subsequently be called into question, have formed panels of, typically, three external IFA firms from which clients, in their ignorance, are invited to choose. Some firms have even ignored the overriding requirement for independence and have established relations with sales organisations which avoid the FSA restriction against describing themselves as independent by using the description 'wealth managers', and whose salesmen (euphemistically called 'partners') seem to be in denial as to their true status.

The overriding requirement, of course, is that client referrals should only be made to IFAs, i.e. advisers who are not tied to one or more individual product providers, but are able to access the whole of the product market on behalf of their clients. Rule 19 of the Solicitors' Code of Conduct 2007, which deals with financial services, reiterates the core duty laid down in subrule 1.03, that: 'independence is a core duty' and states in subrule 19.01(1) that 'you must not, in connection with any regulated activity':

(b) have any arrangement with other persons under which you could be constrained to recommend to clients or effect for them (or refrain from doing so) transactions:

    (i)   in some investments but not others;
    (ii) with some persons but not others; or
    (iii) through the agency of some persons but not others . . .

The mischief addressed by the requirement for independence goes beyond the desirability of being able to access the whole of the market, and reflects the fact that financial advisers who are contracted to represent one or more product providers are remunerated by commission paid by the companies they represent and the quid pro quo for their accepting this 'tie' is that the rates of commission they receive are substantially inflated. They are in fact salesmen for the product providers concerned and they do not get paid if they do not succeed in selling product. Consequently, their ability to put the interests of the client first is severely compromised.

To assist solicitors to identify independent financial advisers who share solicitors' ethical principles, SIFA has established a Directory of professional financial advisers which can be accessed via the website **www.sifa-professional.info**. This is confined to financial advisers who:

- are being independent and able to address the whole of the product market on behalf of their clients;
- are directly authorised by the FSA (thereby avoiding the influence of IFA networks);
- possess advanced qualifications; and

- subscribe to a Client Charter which reflects the terms of the Solicitors' Code of Conduct 2007 in relation to remuneration.

The Directory permits solicitors to search for IFA firms by reference to location, specialisation, qualifications and charges. The firms listed are both national and local and include both those which are able to provide specialist advice on a one-off basis and those which provide a more general service and might be receptive to joint ventures or other forms of association.

4

In-house financial services, hive-offs and joint ventures

Ian Muirhead

Solicitors' in-house financial services

The appeal of the in-house proposition lies in the natural synergy which exists between certain types of legal and financial services work and the accessibility of an in-house adviser for client meetings and internal discussions.

However, despite the advantages enjoyed by authorised professional firms in being exempted from the Financial Services Compensation Scheme and the EU capital adequacy requirements (see Chapter 1), the number of Financial Services Authority (FSA)-authorised law firms has declined over the years and now represents less than 1 per cent of the profession. From the outset, when the Law Society became a recognised professional body in the late 1980s, only about 20 per cent of firms evinced any interest in the practice development opportunity offered by financial services, and of those which proceeded to employ a financial adviser many failed to integrate the service with the firm's mainstream activities or to entrust their clients to advisers whose work they did not understand and whose ethical standards they suspected might be different from their own. Consequently, many in-house financial advisers were regarded as second-class citizens and left to fend for themselves, and when heavy duty regulation was introduced by the FSA in 2001 and stock markets were in decline, firms made for the exit, disillusioned by increasing costs and declining income.

In a small number of cases, effective integration has been achieved and in-house financial services units have flourished, and the regular contact which is the basis of financial advisers' relationships with clients has proved helpful in maintaining solicitors' own client relations. However, there have also been disadvantages to the in-house model. Solicitors have often been uncomfortable with the insistence of the FSA that responsibility for regulatory compliance should be undertaken by a partner or director rather than by the financial adviser who is clearly likely to have the best understanding of the requirements. In-house financial advisers, for their part, have had to shoulder responsibility for administration and IT systems which have proved to be incompatible with those of the law firm. A further disadvantage is that in-house financial advisers have until now been denied partner status and some have resented the fact that they have been building up a saleable capital asset in which they have had no share.

Some of these issues have now been alleviated by the arrival of legal disciplinary practices (LDPs), but they have nevertheless prompted a significant number of authorised professional firms to hive off their financial services into separate units; and a number of authorised firms, when converting to limited liability partnership (LLP) status, have taken the opportunity to obtain authorisation for a hive off rather than applying for fresh FSA authorisation in the name of the LLP. It is notable, however, that it has been the accountancy firms, which have been significantly more successful than solicitors in financial services, which have undertaken the greatest number of hive offs, even though the question of partner status has not been an issue for them.

Hiving off the in-house solicitors' financial services unit

A firm hiving off its financial services unit would normally relinquish its own FSA authorisation and would time this to coincide with the completion of the authorisation of the hive-off, which would be expected to take at least three months and would involve an FSA fee of £1,500 (for a 'simple' application). The authorisation process is complicated and most firms enlist the guidance of a compliance consultant, whose fee would also need to be taken into account. The process for obtaining FSA authorisation is explained in the SIFA Compliance Manual. It would of course be possible to avoid this process by simply selling the financial services business to another FSA-authorised firm, and this has been done on a number of occasions, with the vendor receiving a special class of shares by way of consideration.

The question of the relative shareholdings in a hived-off business, as between the partners in the parent firm and the IFAs, is likely to give rise to lively debate, and it is necessary to distinguish between, on the one hand, the value which has been contributed by each of the participants in establishing the business (reflecting their past input or effort) and, on the other hand, the future contribution to be made in growing the business. The proprietorial instinct of many partners in parent firms leads them to expect that the business should remain theirs, whereas the reality is that post hive-off they may no longer be providing the business support infrastructure and are likely to be little more than back-seat drivers and ongoing referrers of clients. The people whose drive will dictate the future success of the business are the IFAs.

From this point of view, and having regard to the desirability of providing an incentive to the financial advisers who will be running the business, there is an argument for giving the IFAs the controlling shareholding, though such is the relative bargaining position that few IFAs achieve this in practice. Some, having been stymied in their efforts to secure what they considered an appropriate percentage shareholding, have simply walked out and set up shop independently, and there has been little that the solicitors have been able to do to prevent clients from following them.

Another factor in favour of giving control of a hive-off to the IFAs is that if a financial adviser firm is known locally to be controlled by a particular professional firm, then even if the hive-off operates under a completely different name, it may find it difficult to attract referrals from other firms. This would undermine what is often a key objective of a hive-off, namely to address the local professional market beyond the clientele of the parent firm so as to be able to achieve greater critical mass as a basis for increased specialisation and investment in administrative facilities.

One way of overcoming any reluctance on the part of other firms to refer their clients would be to invite the participation from one or more firms *ab initio*, in the form of either shareholdings or a share incentive scheme, so that the hive-off was seen to have become a common external financial services resource in the locality. SIFA has a model for this arrangement, which involves adopting the name and marketing get-up of Professional Financial Centres.

Consideration will need to be given to the manner in which shares in a hive-off should be held by the partners in the parent firm. Bearing in mind the frequency with which partnerships change, it is unlikely to be appropriate to issue shares to individuals. Instead, they could be held on trust or even by a separate company. If the parent firm is to have the controlling stake in the hive-off, then the issue will arise that the revenues received from the hive-off will be taxed on an associated company basis.

When the hive-off is ready to commence business, the parent firm should write to its clients advising them of the change of structure, introducing the newly hived-off organisation, reassuring the clients of continuity of service and requesting approval for the transfer of their files (see Precedent E). Product supply 'agencies' would also have to be transferred. The firm's letter might suitably enclose an introductory letter from the IFA firm and a copy of its corporate marketing material.

Experience to date suggests that a financial advice business is usually most suitably run by financial advisers and does not sit comfortably within a traditional professional practice. However, new forms of practice may well emerge, of which financial services will be an integral part, when the professional 'Big Bang' resulting from the Legal Services Act 2007 takes place in 2011 or 2012, and the canny Scots have already provided a template for a legal and financial boutique, or 'family office'. As Douglas

Connell, the Joint Managing Partner of Edinburgh law firm Turcan Connell commented in The Lawyer in November 2005:

> You cannot adequately advise a private client of means on succession planning without detailed legal knowledge. But you also need to have expertise in pensions and tax planning.

Joint ventures

An arrangement which is finding increasing favour with both solicitors and IFA firms is the formation of a joint venture (JV), i.e. a financial service unit which is separate from both firms and in which both firms have a financial and business interest. There are several advantages in such an arrangement.

The first advantage is that the solicitors are relieved of responsibility for compliance and management. These can be delegated to the IFA firm. The second advantage is that the solicitors are likely to have a greater degree of commitment and involvement in the success of the joint company than they would if they were simply referring clients to an IFA firm in which they had no proprietorial interest. The third advantage is that, as with any solicitors' separate business, they can conveniently be remunerated for their involvement by means of dividend and this can suitably be calculated by reference to the value of the client referrals. The compliance requirement here is laid down by subrule 21.05 of the Solicitors' Code of Conduct 2007, which states:

> if you or your firm refer(s) a client to the separate business, the client must first be informed of your interest in the separate business, that the separate business is not regulated by the Solicitors Regulation Authority, and that the statutory protections attaching to clients of a lawyer regulated by the Authority are not available to clients of the separate business . . .

If a JV were formed with an existing IFA business as partner, the best way of achieving FSA authorisation would be for the IFA to make the JV its 'appointed representative' (AR). The IFA firm would then be responsible to the FSA for the JV's compliance with FSA rules, which from a practical point of view would necessitate its installing the same procedures and systems in the JV – including IT systems – as its own. A simple Heads of Terms for a JV is shown as Precedent I.

Rule 21 of the Solicitors' Code of Conduct 2007 specifically permits solicitors' separate businesses to be ARs, but only of independent financial adviser firms. However, the AR arrangement is not available to law firms in respect of their in-house financial services units. Subrule 19.01 of the Code prohibits any English or Welsh law firm from being an AR for investment business and the Law Society of Scotland takes a similar line. The Institute of Chartered Accountants, by contrast, permits its member firms to be ARs of independent or whole-of-market adviser firms but not of tied sales organisations (Statement 1.208 of the Institute's Ethical Guidance).

The capital adequacy requirements of the FSA would hold no horrors for the JV. The FSA does not impose specific capital adequacy requirements on ARs, but principals are required to ensure that ARs are financially stable. ARs have their own FSA authorisation numbers but would be covered by their principals' professional indemnity policies, in which they should be named.

Decisions as to the name of a JV would depend on the marketing plans. If the intention was to market mainly to the clients of the law firm, then advantage might well be taken of the removal, in rule 21 of the Code, of the bar on solicitors' separate businesses adopting names similar to those of the firms in which the participating solicitors practise. The new provision reads simply:

> the separate business must not be held out or described in such a way as to suggest that the separate business is carrying on a practice regulated by the Solicitors Regulation Authority, or that any lawyer connected with your firm is providing services through the separate business as a practising lawyer regulated by the Solicitors Regulation Authority . . .

The first solicitor/IFA JV to benefit from the relaxation was East Anglia-based Kester Cunningham John Financial Planning, a joint venture between Kester Cunningham John Solicitors and PB Financial Planning, the IFA arm of Price Bailey Chartered Accountants.

Discussing the advantages of the JV model, Director Paul Russell remarked

> Business development is not always at the forefront of lawyers' minds and I believe that they would benefit from taking a more commercial view of life, especially in the current climate. In general, IFAs have this ingrained in them, though this should not be taken to imply that they don't put clients first. In my experience the joint venture model works, because I have been able to demonstrate my expertise at the coal face and to bring a degree of commerciality to the way the solicitors operate.

If the intention of the participants were to market the services of the JV to a wider population of clients and to attract business from other professional firms, it would make sense to adopt a neutral name and to house the JV in physically separate premises, preferably outside the immediate locality of the participating law firm.

Some IFA firms which have established JVs with solicitors have opted for a 50/50 shareholding split as between solicitors and IFAs, while others have provided for the solicitors to own 100 per cent of the shares in the JV and for the IFA firm to be appointed as manager. The 100 per cent arrangement has appeal because it avoids the need for the negotiation of shareholder rights, which can slow down and can even scupper proposed relationships.

The shareholders' agreement would provide for the IFA principal to retain such proportion of the income of the JV as was required to recover the cost of the compliance, administrative and advisory services provided and their agreed share of the profit. The JV could recruit its own financial advisers, but it would probably be preferable in most cases for the IFA participant to second its own advisers to the JV, so that the JV would have access to the full range of specialist skills available from the IFA firm. The advisers would in this situation be registered with the FSA as being 'approved persons' for both organisations. Clearly, from the point of view of the allocation of revenue, this necessitates the JV having systems which enable it accurately to identify each client as a client of either the IFA firm or the JV. These systems would also show the income derived from each client and the identity of the solicitor who had referred the client.

Solicitor firms would normally wish to notify their clients that a separate business had been formed to service their financial advice needs and might do so by sending a circular letter which would include the warning statements required by subrule 21.05 of the Code and might suitably enclose a marketing leaflet for the JV such as that shown as Precedent F. Precedent G is a letter referring an individual client to a JV.

5

Tax and accounting considerations

Jon Cartwright

Choosing a business vehicle

A decision will need to be made as to the most appropriate vehicle for any form of joint financial services firm formed by solicitors and independent financial advisers (IFAs). The choice is usually between a limited company and a limited liability partnership (LLP).

Limited companies are the traditional business structure, with the advantage of familiarity and perceived ease of disposal compared to other structures. However, limited companies can often be less flexible than a partnership structure so far as ownership is concerned, and the tax regime attaching to smaller companies is becoming less favourable.

Areas of tax difficulty or cost with limited companies which do not apply to partnerships are as follows:

- Incoming and outgoing owners have to buy and sell shares in the company. These shares therefore have to be valued, and there will always be a taxation incidence.
- There is no mechanism to pass ownership of shares to employees at a considerable discount, or even for no payment, without an (often heavy) income tax charge arising.
- Her Majesty's Revenue and Customs (HMRC) is gradually tightening up on owner remuneration techniques which avoid paying employer's National Insurance, which is a considerable potential cost.
- There is no straightforward way of varying the profit sharing arrangements of owners in different years without incurring expensive National Insurance costs. The typical solution is to create differing share classes, which, though easy enough to set up, may not always provide what is required for the longer term.
- The provision of benefits – for example the running costs of owners' cars – cannot be provided without expensive tax and National Insurance liabilities arising.

On the positive side so far as taxation is concerned, unincorporated IFA businesses which change to limited company status can benefit from what can be considerable tax savings in the first few years post-incorporation, as a result of selling their goodwill to the new company and subsequently withdrawing the proceeds from the company free of tax.

LLPs are the more recent option, having been available only since 2001. The key point with LLPs is that they are a separate legal entity in the same way as a limited company and therefore offer limited liability protection, but they are taxed as if they were a general partnership.

From a tax point of view this can offer considerable advantages, predominantly the freedom from the shackles of the potentially complex and expensive world of both corporation and employee tax which, when taken together, can prove expensive for many corporates. Also, LLPs can alter ownership and profit sharing arrangements much more easily than companies.

There is no easy rule of thumb to recommend one form of structure over the other, as each case really does need to be considered on its own merits. It is interesting to note that businesses are now setting up as combinations of limited companies and LLPs, in order to extract the best parts of each. There could be an argument against making the joint venture a limited company if the participating IFA firm were also a limited company, because this could trigger tax consequences arising from the provisions for associated companies, and in this situation it might be better to arrange for the JV to be an LLP.

Valuing a financial services business

In many cases the vehicle for a joint financial services venture will be an existing IFA unit, whether this be a separate firm or an in-house unit, and it will be necessary to place a value on this unit. The valuation will generally centre around a combination of: assets base; quality of clients; recurring and non-recurring fee income; and profitability.

Subject to prevailing economic conditions, IFA businesses can command significant value, given that they tend to have a recurring income stream from the same clients. Contrast this with solicitors' practices, where a reasonable proportion of the work consists of one-off assignments.

Generally speaking, larger IFAs will achieve greater valuation multiples than smaller ones, but of the 10,000 or so IFA businesses in the UK the vast majority have fewer than three advisers. Consolidation is happening, but it is a fairly slow process, albeit aided by an ageing IFA population (the average age of principals is understood to be around 54).

Whilst there are numerous methods which can be used to value an IFA business, the two most common focus on future achievable turnover and profitability.

Turnover-based valuations

Turnover-based valuations necessitate determining the most appropriate turnover figure. The headline turnover figure may not take account of client commission/fee rebates, and the net figure must be agreed.

Whilst prior year turnover figures are important to consider, what really matters is where the business is heading, i.e. what is the anticipated future attainable net turnover figure? The prospective purchaser needs to have a realistic eye when considering this, particularly in smaller IFA businesses where people changes, particularly owners retiring or moving on, can have a considerable impact.

When mapping this out, fee income must be separated from commissions, and initial commission from trail income, as the make-up here will influence the turnover multiple.

As might be expected, higher multiples will attach to businesses with a higher proportion of fee income compared to commissions, and when looking at commissions, a higher level of trail compared to up-front income.

Turning to the actual valuation multiple, a common range is 1.5 to 3 times future maintainable net turnover. Larger IFAs will achieve a higher multiple than smaller ones, as also will those with higher quality clients. Occasionally a valuation might be up to five times net turnover, but this would be rare. On retirement sales the multiple might be as low as a figure of 1 times, or even less.

It is important not to underestimate the importance of intangible assets such as a well-maintained database, robust systems, regular diarised reviews with clients, etc.

Other factors that will be influential are:

- location and socio-economic area;
- age and length of service of staff and owners;
- competition;
- security of tenure;
- value of name and reputation, i.e. brand;
- any niche work areas.

It is interesting to note that the staff of the IFA business are unlikely to have any direct bearing on the valuation, even though they are the heart and soul of the business. Negotiating lock-in arrangements with key people will, however, boost the value, or could sometimes break the deal.

Earnings-based valuations

Earnings-based valuations have as their starting point what is generally referred to as 'earnings [profits] before interest and tax' (EBIT). Once an appropriate EBIT figure has been determined, a suitable multiple can be applied to it.

As with the turnover-based method of valuation, it is the future maintainable EBIT figure that is the important one. Clearly, past performance will be a guide here but known future factors must be taken into account.

When looking at EBIT figures for prior years, the first thing which needs to be done is to adjust the historically reported profit figures for all factors which may have made them a non-commercial figure in the first place. To explain:

- Owners of IFA businesses may tend to pay themselves principally via dividends if they operate via limited companies, or drawings if they are sole traders or partnerships. Either way, these do not feature as an expense in the profit and loss account, as they are a distribution of profit. A realistic commercial salary must therefore be factored in for the individual or individuals, and deducted from the reported profit.
- The owners may own the trading premises, and allow the business to use it without paying a commercial rent. If so, an imputed rent figure needs to be deducted from profits.
- Owners' car running costs may go through the business, and need to be partly or fully added back to profits, as will any other owner perks that would not normally be provided for individuals undertaking that role in the business. There may also be spouses' wages and other similar items to add back.

Once an adjusted profit figure has been arrived at for prior years, detailed attention must be turned to considering how this is likely to change in the future, and a view taken as to likely maintainable future profits.

Then, as with the turnover method, consideration must be given to the multiple which is to be applied. A typical range might be 4 to 6, but this depends greatly on the variables set out in the turnover valuation referred to above.

Asset-based valuation methods

Asset-based valuation methods crop up in theory more than they do in practice. What is meant here is the value of clients' financial assets under management as opposed to assets of the business. The principal difficulty is knowing what funds the IFA business does have under management; and funds can be quite transient.

Here again, robust back office systems with good management information can be very helpful. Additionally, more IFA businesses are moving investments on to 'Wrap' platforms, whereby portfolios are managed online. This enables any prospective purchaser to identify more easily the income stream derived from these assets. If this method is being used, a suitable multiple may be in the range of between 1 and 3 per cent, again depending on all of the factors mentioned above.

If, however, there were no database of clients and no records of renewals, and if a lot of work needed to be done by the acquirer, then the value of the business might be considered not to justify any up-front payment, but to be a function purely of future earnings. So renewals might in this situation suitably be paid to the owners quarterly in arrears over the succeeding three or four years. Transparency would be maintained after the sale by operating separate bank accounts and sharing commission statements. The sellers would of course retain the income from business conducted before the date of the transfer.

The value which may be attached to clientele is often debatable, because in many cases the frequency and regularity of contact which financial services involves will have resulted in the client's allegiance switching from the referring solicitor or accountant to the financial adviser and consequently the client will in practice often wish to follow the IFA to a new firm despite any non-competition restrictions in his or her terms of employment. So in the final analysis the IFA may have the whip hand.

There is a widespread assumption that goodwill enjoys favourable treatment for capital gains tax. In the hands of the recipient of proceeds from the sale of goodwill, this is the case, given the introduction of the flat rate of capital gains tax of 18 per cent with effect from 6 April 2008, and the possibility of achieving an effective 10 per cent capital gains tax rate if a claim is likely to be made for entrepreneurs' relief (the replacement for taper relief). However, if considered from the point of view of the tax position of the seller and the purchaser together, attributing consideration to goodwill does not always achieve the most beneficial situation; and limited companies are in a different position from partnerships.

Other methods

There are a number of other possibilities, but the only one worth mentioning here is the earn-out. Here, a lower initial consideration is agreed for the business, followed by additional consideration in the one to three years post-sale, payable only if certain pre-defined financial targets are met. These targets will generally centre around net turnover and profits, and very often targets for both have to be achieved in order to trigger the earn-out payments.

Earn-outs can be very useful tools, as they take away much of the uncertainty that the purchaser will have over whether income and profits may wane post acquisition, particularly if a previous owner leaves the business or goes part-time. From experience, however, an earn-out can be quite challenging to document in writing, though this is clearly vital. An experienced commercial solicitor is required.

Finally, it will be of concern to the new participants in the hived-off business that they should not become responsible for any liabilities incurred prior to the hive-off transaction, and that the firm from which the hive-off is taking place should have appropriate run-off PI insurance cover.

Valuing part of an IFA business

Given the incidence of joint ventures between solicitors and IFAs, and accountants for that matter, the need may arise to value part of an IFA business as opposed to all of it. This is not always as easy as taking a rateable percentage of the value of the whole.

If the IFA business operates as a limited company, the valuation will generally be influenced by the wording of the Articles of Association, which may require a valuer to place a discount on the value of part of the business compared to the whole, particularly if the part being valued does not carry control, i.e. it amounts to 50 per cent or less.

These discounts can be significant in certain circumstances, but the Articles can of course be re-drafted to suit, subject to shareholder approval. Discounts will rarely apply in partnership situations, or quasi partnerships for that matter.

6

Legal aspects of joint ventures and share schemes

Steve Hartley

Objectives of joint ventures

Law firms which wish to go beyond a simple client referral arrangement with an external independent financial adviser (IFA) and to create a joint venture (JV) may consider either establishing a relationship with an existing IFA firm which is able to offer equity participation, or setting up a new IFA business which would be part-owned by the law firm and an existing IFA business, and which would be managed by and derive its Financial Services Authority (FSA) authorisation from the existing IFA business, as its 'appointed representative'.

The expectation would normally be that a new IFA firm would be confined to the business generated by the participating law firm, and might bear its name, whereas an existing IFA firm which offered share participation to local professional firms generally, and might have been established specifically to act as a common resource for such firms, would benefit from having access to a wider client base. IFA firms known to be closely associated with a particular professional firm would be less likely to be able to attract business from other firms, who might be jealous of their clients' loyalty or might perceive potential conflicts of interest.

The advantages of both types of JV arrangement are that they enable the law firm to provide a wider client service without having to assume responsibility for compliance and management, and to benefit from the income generated from clients referred to the JV and from the future growth of the JV itself. In both cases, the participating professional firm will be keen to retain and protect its proprietorship of clients transferred to the JV.

Careful consideration must therefore be given to the structure of the arrangements:

• The first and foremost consideration will be to ring-fence the value of any clients referred to the JV and to secure the benefit of the growth in such value.

- Consideration will also need to be given to what should happen to the income derived from those clients, bearing in mind on the one hand the need to fund the day-to-day running of the JV and to pay and incentivise the management team, and on the other hand the need to return to the law firm some share of the income derived from any clients referred to the JV.
- Any firm considering participation will also be eager to clearly ringfence the value in any clients transferred to the JV and the income received by the JV in respect of those clients.
- The participating professional firms will almost certainly also wish to benefit from any capital growth in the JV as a whole.
- The JV's management team will wish to be rewarded in terms of income but will also wish to participate in any capital value growth generated by their efforts. Consequently, it will be important to determine the most appropriate management structure.

Incentivising and rewarding participants

The question of incentivising and rewarding participants requires particular attention in cases where an IFA firm has been established by a single professional firm ('the founding firm'), perhaps by hiving off its own in-house financial services unit, but the intention is to attract business from other professional firms. In this situation two particular approaches might be considered:

- The JV could allot non-voting preference shares to the founding firm and other participating firms, each firm receiving its own class of preference shares. Preference shares would commonly carry a right to receive periodic income in the form of a preferential dividend, and this could be calculated on an agreed formula, based on income derived from referrals made to the JV by each firm. As a result, the preferential dividend receivable by firms would reflect pro rata the contribution made by each firm when its clients are transferred into the JV.
- Alternatively or in addition, each class of preference shares could carry an additional right to participate in a return of capital on any future realisation of the JV, in the form of a sale of its share capital or a majority of its assets. For example in the event of a realisation, an agreed percentage of the consideration receivable on the sale would be shared between the holders of each class of preference shares. Any balance of the consideration remaining to be distributed after the payment of this preferential return of capital would then be distributed pro rata between the holders of the ordinary (voting/management) shares in the JV. Extreme care would be needed to ensure that the relationship

between the different classes of preference shareholders and the ordinary shareholders was set out clearly and unequivocally.

The issue of preference shares would probably, however, only be appropriate in the case of the founding firm or where a firm with a substantial financial services client database is interested in becoming a participating firm.

Consideration will need to be given regarding to whom ordinary (voting) shares should be allotted. To provide an appropriate incentive, the management team of the JV would be most likely to receive a substantial percentage of the ordinary shares. This would encourage them to grow the business in order to participate in dividends on those shares (after the preference dividends had been paid) and to share in the increase in the capital value of the JV.

A more difficult question is whether and to what extent the founding firm and major participating firms should also receive ordinary shares. In principle it would be right that they should do so, as their clients provide the basis of the value of the JV. However, in practice this might deter other firms from participating. In addition, their contributions might already have been reflected in the issue of preference shares. There is a difficult balance to be struck here between the respective interests of the management team, the founder firm and the participating firms.

The creation of a new class of shares, giving participating solicitors rights to income in the form of dividends and the prospect of a capital return in the event of a third party disposal, may seem attractive at first sight since it involves no immediate outlay of cash on the part of the IFA, and has a capital value upside for the solicitor. However, it is not without its complications, the principal one being taxation.

The taxation issue stems from the fact that new share issues need to be valued, and if the solicitor receives shares in lieu of a cash incentive, there will generally be a tax charge on the market value of the shares at the time of issue. One could consider an argument that the shares in question should only be valued at par on the basis that they have restricted rights, e.g. no voting rights. However, in reality this is unlikely to wash with the HMRC Valuation Office. In addition to this, as and when the shares are sold in the future, the gain arising is unlikely to attract the new entrepreneurs' relief from capital gains tax (which is a pity as it would probably have qualified for the old taper relief), and therefore the mainstream 18 per cent rate of capital gains tax is likely to apply.

As an alternative to issuing ordinary shares to the management team, the founding firm could consider introducing a share option scheme, perhaps geared to the value of business generated by the participating firm. This would have the advantage that the founding firm and the participating firms would retain control of the business of the JV, but the downside would be that the management team would not be able to share in dividends on ordinary shares declared before they exercised their options.

Share options for employees would be designed to enable them to acquire shares in the JV at the end of a defined option period. There are several categories of share schemes – EMI schemes, unapproved schemes and approved schemes. Each has a differing format and tax consequences and detailed advice is needed as to which might be most suitable in any given set of circumstances.

The proposals so far discussed with a view to incentivising participation have focused on benefits in the medium to longer term, in the form of dividends, preferential rights to returns of capital on sale and share options. However, one additional incentive to participate which could be used is to give participating firms greater day-to-day involvement in the management of the JV, without actually providing them with a voice in the form of a right to vote. It would be possible to introduce a threshold whereby participating firms which accounted for an agreed percentage of the business referred into the JV could become entitled to appoint a non-executive director to the board of the JV. Any non-executive directors so appointed would be entitled to attend board meetings and to receive copies of all board minutes and other board papers but, crucially, not to vote. The benefit to the relevant participating firms would be that they would be able to more directly monitor their own interests.

Limited companies as vehicles for joint ventures

Clearly the rights attaching to the various classes of shares need to be laid down in carefully drafted Articles of Association. However, any other rights, powers and restrictions agreed between the various shareholders might suitably be set out in the shareholders' agreement between the parties. The fundamental benefit of a shareholders' agreement is that it offers a position of clarity and an agreed starting point between the founders and the participating firms, to which any future participating firms would be required to subscribe as a pre-condition of membership.

An additional advantage in having a shareholders' agreement is that it permits privacy between the participants. The Articles of Association, and any changes to them, must be registered at the Companies Registry and as such can be inspected by anyone who wishes to do so. Shareholders' agreements, by contrast, are rarely public documents.

The shareholders' agreement would usually be between the management team, the founding firm and the participating firms, and would cover issues such as the following:

- The object and scope of the JV in greater detail than set out in the Memorandum of Association. It can act as 'heads of terms', to document and put into focus the collective goals of the shareholders. The agreement could incorporate reference to a business plan, thus giving the JV an unanimously agreed framework against which to perform.
- The initial capitalisation and funding contributions of the parties, together with details of any commitments, binding or conditional, to make future contributions. Contributions might be financial or might take other forms, such as the provision of intellectual property rights, know-how, secondment of staff or provision of premises.
- Reference to any matters on which decisions can only be made if a defined proportion of the shareholders or any class of shareholders agree. Such matters are often referred to as 'reserved matters' and provide veto rights to minority or class shareholders. Reserved matters could include, inter alia, making amendments to the Memorandum or Articles of Association, altering class rights, allotting shares, making material changes to the business of the JV and declaring any dividends.
- An explanation of how the directors will conduct day-to-day operations of the business. Will there be any other matters on which decisions can only be made if a specified percentage of the shareholders agree, e.g. entering into material contracts, borrowing money or giving security or selling material assets?
- The transfer of shares and when transfers would be permitted; when they would be transferable subject to a right of pre-emption of the other shareholders or class of shareholders; or whether there should be a blanket prohibition on any transfer of shares from the date on which a shareholder is registered as such.
- Whether the holders of a majority of the shares in the JV who might wish to sell the entire issued share capital of the company should be able to require all other shareholders to sell their shares on no less favourable terms ('drag along rights').
- Whether the shareholders should be subject to any restrictive covenants (including non-competition with the JV) both whilst they are shareholders and for an agreed defined period after their ceasing to be shareholders.
- Deadlock mechanisms for the resolution of disputes between the shareholders.
- Criteria for the appointment of directors by the shareholders.

Limited liability partnerships as vehicles for joint ventures

There could be some advantages in adopting a limited liability partnership (LLP) rather than a company as the vehicle for the JV. The members would similarly enjoy limited liability and each member would be liable to tax on their share of the profits.

An LLP will usually be governed by a detailed agreement which deals with many of the matters contained in the Articles of Association and shareholders' agreement of a private company. The LLP agreement would cover constitutional issues and would regulate the relationship between the members, the designated members and the LLP itself. An LLP agreement is a private document between the members and does not require any registration nor will the public have any right to see it.

If a financial services JV were operated via an LLP, the LLP agreement would set out how firms would become members; how the profits, losses and capital growth would be apportioned; and who would become designated members. It would also provide a mechanism for the cessation, voluntary or otherwise, of membership.

Because of its very flexible nature the LLP agreement can contain any agreed structure dealing with both membership and management and in the present context the objectives already discussed, involving the use of preference shares and ordinary shares, can easily be achieved by creating different classes of membership with different profit, income and capital growth sharing arrangements, different entrance and exit routes and different rights in relation to day-to-day operations.

The management team would be likely to be the members with principal operational responsibilities and control, but the founding firm and any participating firms with a significant interest in the JV would be likely to have rights to appoint 'management members' and/or to attend meetings of the 'management members', which would be denied to other participating firms. All members would be entitled to receive copies of the LLP accounts and to attend, if not to vote at, general meetings of the members. As with a limited company, this would give the ordinary members a greater sense of cohesion and involvement without taking control away from the 'management members'.

In considering the rights appropriate for each class of membership, careful attention would be required to avoid certain default provisions that apply under the regulations that bind LLPs. Examples would be the provision that all members are entitled to vote at members' meetings and the provision that all members are agents of the partnership and therefore entitled to bind the partnership. The LLP agreement would therefore state the rights attaching to each class of membership, whilst also considering which default rights they would not have. In much the same way as described above, it would also specify which matters should be reserved for the decision of a certain class of membership and which proportion of those members would be required to approve a proposed action.

By creating a combination of classes of membership, it would be possible both to establish a suitable management structure for the LLP and to incentivise the participants as well as the management team.

The LLP agreement would also deal with other provisions commonly found in shareholder agreements. For example, a provision containing a mechanism for members to sell or transfer their interest in the LLP, including any suitable blanket prohibitions on transfers or, at the other end of the scale, any transfers which would be permitted without being subject to a pre-emption process.

Termination provisions would also be addressed. The default position is that a member cannot be expelled from an LLP against his wishes unless there is express provision to do so. When membership ceases, whether by retirement or expulsion, that member's involvement in the management or administration of the business of the LLP must also cease. The LLP agreement could include a mechanism by which membership may be terminated and, where appropriate, how any outstanding financial entitlements would be distributed to the outgoing member. Thereafter, the LLP agreement would set out any post-termination restrictive covenants whether in favour of the outgoing member or the LLP and the continuing members including, for example, the future use of any client details.

7

Alternative business structures

Peter Gamson

Many people view legal disciplinary practices as a transitional business model and consider alternative business structures (ABSs), which are likely to become reality in 2011 or 2012, as the cornerstone of the 'economic' elements of the Legal Services Act 2007. From the perspective of those interested in becoming involved in ABSs, the main benefits should be:

- Increased flexibility: non-legal firms, including those involved in financial services, insurance, accountancy, banks and estate agents will have the freedom to develop synergies with firms of solicitors (or other lawyers) by forming ABS firms and offering integrated legal and other professional services.
- Increased access to finance: at present, business owners face constraints on the amount of equity, mainly debt equity, which they can raise.
- It should be easier for ABSs to acquire and retain high quality non-legal staff, particularly if they are rewarded in the same way as legal staff.
- New service providers in the marketplace will be best placed to bring about innovations and price reductions. Many observers perceive much inefficiency in the way that legal services are provided, and the government hopes that the Act will lead to greater access to more affordable legal services.

ABSs will permit the involvement of private equity, which should provide a further catalyst for change. Investors' perception appears to be that the legal services sector exhibits poor service delivery, inadequate quality, too much cost and insufficient profit. The aims of these investors are likely to be to get rid of over-resourcing and strip out inefficiency. They are likely to consider the improvements to added value which can be delivered both by lawyers and by systems improvements, and will no doubt weigh up factors such as the durability, in the face of critical opinion, of the reservation of litigation services to solicitors (which is currently preserved by the Legal Services Act 2007).

Of course, there is a precedent for ABSs in that several of the then big five accounting firms created multi-disciplinary practices (MDPs) in the late 1990s and early 2000s which were eventually downscaled or abandoned, despite being simple in concept and reflecting all the positive aspects referred to above. This invites the question of why these early attempts at accountancy-based MDPs failed.

Garrets (Andersens), Klegal (KPMG), Landwell (PricewaterhouseCoopers (PWC)), Deloitte Legal and Tite and Lewis (originally PWC and then Ernst & Young) were established in the belief that providing clients with a full range of complementary business advisory and legal services would generate higher revenues as clients using the advisory firm would then wish to use the associated law firm. In many cases this provided a powerful proposition to a client – the ultimate one stop shop, and notably in the case of Landwell, this arrangement continues to flourish today. However, these arrangements are not without their difficulties.

As with the simple client referral relationship, working within an MDP reduces the prospects for the referral of work by competitor firms. Now that KPMG is no longer involved in what was KLegal, it is highly unlikely that when looking for a legal firm to which to refer its core clients, it would choose Landwell. Instead, it would be likely to use to one of the many independent law firms that are not tied to its competitor. Furthermore, when these MDPs were originally established, they were founded in the belief that the major proportion of their revenue would arise via internal referrals and work from the advisory firm's existing clients. In making this assumption, the strength and depth of referral relationships built up by partners over a number of years had not been fully considered.

A senior partner in these advisory firms might typically have built up a significant network of highly capable and specialist external contacts, knowing exactly to whom he should refer work in order to ensure that his client received the best advice in each area of advice. No doubt, in return, he would have expected to receive a number of in-bound referrals and, over the years, whilst some relationships would have changed and others fallen away, the quality relationships would have endured.

If an accountancy-based firm had created an MDP, its partners would have been expected to refer their future work to the lawyers within the tied law firm, despite the fact that the individuals involved might be people of whom they had no prior knowledge or experience and despite the fact that they might have made substantial efforts to establish effective and trustful working relationships elsewhere. Ultimately, the understandable reluctance which might arise could create a significant hurdle to the success of such MDPs, and there might well be similar resistance within any legal or accountancy firm introducing a team of independent financial advisers (IFAs) to work alongside their professionals in an MDP model.

Another critical aspect of the MDP is how the ultimate client might view the prospect of the various professional inputs being provided from the same source. Whilst it would present a conveniently comprehensive service which many private clients would undoubtedly find extremely appealing, some larger private and corporate clients might question whether they would be receiving the most specialised IFA advice. To avoid this becoming a major issue, it is vital that the IFAs are appropriately understood and marketed by the other professionals so that clients feel they are being provided with the best service rather than the most expedient.

Times have changed since the MDP experiment of the big five accountancy practices, and their precedent may be less applicable at the local or regional level. One certainty is that the trend towards consolidation within the legal profession will continue, as firms strive to achieve critical mass and economies of scale as a defence against the greatly increased levels of competition which they are bound to encounter; and this is likely to give rise to an increase in the cross-fertilisation of professional disciplines. However, the main impetus for change may well come from outside the legal profession.

Tax planning

8

Financial solutions for estate planning

Dave Robinson

This section of the handbook summarises some of the insurance and investment-based financial solutions which may be considered as a complement to solicitors' and accountants' mainstream advice in the field of estate planning. A more detailed description of each arrangement can be found in the SIFA handbook *Financial Solutions for Estate Planning*.

The solutions covered here relate to:

- trust-based gifting strategies;
- investments which are designed to attract business or agricultural property relief;
- life assurance;
- purchased life annuities and 'back-to-back' schemes.

Trust-based gifting strategies

From a tax perspective, insurance bonds or endowment policies are often the most appropriate vehicles for schemes whose underlying investments are cash or income-yielding securities, while collective investment funds are usually more appropriate for growth-oriented investments.

Whichever vehicle is employed, trust-based arrangements are usually based on the well-established 'carve-out' principle, whereby the settlor retains certain rights to capital and/or income which are designed to provide for the settlor's on-going financial security but have little or no value for the purposes of inheritance tax. The settlor's rights are usually retained on a bare trust. Other rights (e.g. death claim values and surrender values) are gifted to trustees for the benefit of persons excluding the settlor.

The arrangements generally share the following characteristics:

- There is no 'settlement' of the policy or investment as a whole. The property which is given to the trustees is the balance of benefits under the policy or investment and the benefit which is retained is not reserved by the donor out of property gifted, but is simply a benefit which is excluded from the gift.

- 'Gift with reservation' issues should not therefore arise in relation to the retained benefit and the arrangement should also not give rise to any charge to pre-owned asset tax.

Although many of the trusts referred to have been designed by insurance and investment companies, it is sometimes possible to utilise these trusts without being confined to the provider's investment products; though in some cases there is a requirement to purchase the provider's insurance bond or collective investment scheme 'tax-wrapper' or its investment management services.

Once a view has been taken as to which, if any, arrangements may suit a client, it will be appropriate to discuss with the client the arguments for and against the alternatives of creating a potentially exempt transfer (PET), a chargeable lifetime transfer (CLT) or a combination of both, before agreeing the form of trust to be used. Most of the trust deeds contain wide administrative powers.

Gifts into trust using insurance bonds

These arrangements usually involve the gifted funds being held within either a UK-based or offshore insurance or a capital redemption bond, both of which generally have the same tax treatment for UK-based investors. A capital redemption bond is essentially a similar vehicle to an insurance bond, but requires no life assured. Most of the major UK insurance companies offer offshore bonds to the UK market from the Isle of Man or Dublin; and both these centres offer a level of investor protection which is broadly similar to that available under the Financial Services Compensation Scheme in respect of UK investments.

Investments held within an insurance or capital redemption bond are generally free of capital gains tax (CGT) but potentially subject to income tax in the hands of UK-based taxpayers. They deny individuals and trustees access to annual CGT allowances but their structure permits them to be used to defer, and therefore potentially reduce, income tax (IT). Bonds can also greatly simplify trust and tax administration.

Arrangements which involve insurance bonds or capital redemption bonds favour investors who stand to benefit from the underlying investments being subject to IT rather than CGT – who usually seek a relatively low-risk investment strategy. Clients who require a more growth-oriented strategy may be better served by a collective fund arrangement, which will be subject to CGT. However, in choosing between the two alternatives it will be necessary to take account of the interests of all parties – the settlor, the trustees and the intended beneficiaries.

The key to the insurance-based arrangements is the facility which these products provide for the investor to withdraw up to 5 per cent of the capital each year, so as to provide what amounts to an income, without any immediate tax consequences. The withdrawal of more than 5 per cent a year would be regarded as a 'chargeable event' and the resulting 'chargeable gain' would be subject to IT – as indeed would the proceeds on the ultimate redemption of the bond. The gain will be assessed on the owner of the bond at the time of redemption and will be calculated by reference to their tax position at the time. However, the assignment of a bond, for example by the settlor to the trustees or by the trustees to a beneficiary, will generally not constitute a chargeable event unless the assignment is for money or money's worth.

If a chargeable event occurs in relation to a bond held within a trust, the charge to IT will generally be assessed on the settlor, if alive and UK resident in the year when the event occurs; and if the settlor is not alive the chargeable gain will be assessed on the trust.

Under the Income Tax (Trading and Other Income) Act 2005, s.538 the settlor has a statutory right to recover from the trustees any IT paid as a result of the chargeable gain. However, it may be unwise to exercise this right because generally the opinion has been expressed by Counsel that doing so could compromise the inheritance tax (IHT) efficiency of the trust.

Most insurance and capital redemption bonds can accommodate single or joint settlors and are structured as a series of identical policy segments. This permits greater flexibility and tax efficiency because each segment can be assigned or encashed individually, without affecting the remaining segments.

The two most popular types of bond-based arrangements, discounted gift trusts and loan schemes, are discussed in Chapter 9.

Gifts into trust using collective investment funds

The principal types of collective investment are unit and investment trusts and open-ended investment companies (OEICs) and, in the same way as with most of the insurance and capital redemption bond-based arrangements, the arrangements which use these forms of 'tax-wrapper' are designed to allow clients to mitigate a potential IHT liability by removing assets from their estate, whilst providing some continued access to capital.

The charges on collective-based plans can be lower than those on insurance bond-based plans, but the more significant distinction is that the capital returns on the underlying investments are subject to CGT rather than

IT. They therefore enable settlors and/or trustees to utilise their annual CGT allowances on disposal and they may offer growth-oriented investors a more favourable tax rate than under the IT regime. They are likely also to be more suitable for settlors with significant capital losses which are available to offset against future gains.

On the other hand, these plans offer no scope for IT deferral – though any charge to IT might potentially be minimised by restricting investment to collective funds which yield little or no income and this approach would also be expected to simplify the trustees' tax reporting responsibilities.

Because the settlor has an interest in the trust via future reversions the settlor is, whilst alive and UK resident, the tax point for any IT which may arise in respect of income returns generated by the underlying investments. However, on account of the removal, with effect from the 2008/09 tax year, of the settlor-interested rules in relation to CGT, it is the trustees who are now the tax point for CGT both during the settlor's lifetime and after his death. Of course, the trustees have their own annual CGT exemption of 50 per cent of the allowance available to individuals – though if offshore trustees had been appointed it would be the settlor's exemption which would apply.

If a settlor has made more than one settlement after 6 June 1978, each settlement which exists at any time during a year of assessment is generally regarded as a qualifying settlement within a group of settlements. In this case the annual CGT exemption available to each set of trustees is restricted by dividing the amount of the trust exemption by the number of settlements in the group, up to a maximum of five settlements. However, each settlement does have its own nil rate band for IHT purposes.

Value remaining in the trust after the death of the settlor may include unrealised capital gains. Such value can be passed to the beneficiaries at the trustees' discretion over more than one tax year. Each transfer creates a chargeable event for CGT purposes but the trustees' unused annual exemption is available to offset the gain. By spreading the distribution to beneficiaries over a number of tax years it may be possible to reduce the ultimate CGT charge.

Business and agricultural property relief

These arrangements generally involve investment in assets which qualify for business property relief (BPR) or agricultural property relief (APR). Their key advantage is the comparatively short two-year holding period qualification period for IHT relief and they may therefore be attractive to clients who are elderly and/or in relatively poor health. They also enable the client to retain direct ownership of the asset and any income stream arising from it.

The main disadvantage is that the underlying investment is restricted to qualifying assets which can involve relatively high risk and/or illiquidity. Recently, however, some new structures have been designed to secure the advantage of tax relief while minimising the risk and liquidity issues.

Generally the arrangements fall into the following categories:

- **Alternative investment market (AIM) portfolios** comprising shares in AIM-listed companies which meet the qualifying criteria for BPR. Most managers emphasise reduction of investment risk as far as possible through investment in companies which have reasonably strong financial positions and track records. Some investment managers now offer a degree of capital protection through the purchase of either an insurance policy or a hedging facility.
- **Enterprise investment schemes** which can also offer clients some potentially useful IT or CGT reliefs in addition to IHT efficiency. Such investments can be quite high-risk and/or illiquid but again some specialist managers try to reduce risk as far as possible by investing in AIM-listed companies or companies with tangible asset backing, or by restricting investment to certain trades or sectors.
- **Trading companies established by investment managers**, in which clients can purchase shares, and which have been specifically created to carry out what are perceived as relatively low-risk, relatively liquid, but BPR-qualifying activities.
- **Forestry or agricultural asset arrangements**, generally involving investment in commercially managed woodland and/or farms. Forestry-based investment can offer potentially useful IT and CGT exempt income and capital growth.

Life insurance

Whether or not a client can obtain a cost-effective life assurance policy will depend upon a number of factors, principally their gender, age, state of health, lifestyle and personal habits (particularly smoking).

Types of policy

Term insurance is relatively low-cost because it is a pure insurance contract with no investment element. Therefore clients who survive beyond the expiry date of the policy will generally not receive any benefit beyond the peace of mind they may have gained during the policy term. In order to remove the sum insured from the client's estate, it is crucial that the policy is arranged under trust for the benefit of their executors or heirs. If no other property is added to the trust and the proceeds of any death claim are distributed promptly by the trustees, it is unlikely that the 'relevant property' provisions will apply.

Gift inter vivos policies, with terms of up to seven years and cover which decreases in line with IHT taper relief, may be considered at the time when a gift of capital is made, so as to cover the potential IHT liability which would arise if death occurred within the qualifying period for IHT relief.

Whole-of-life assurance policies are guaranteed to provide benefits on death whenever it might occur (which is why they are policies of assurance rather than insurance), provided that the premiums are maintained and the policy terms are met. Accordingly, they come at a higher cost, but this also means that, depending upon how the contract is arranged, it may accumulate some degree of surrender value over time, i.e. the policy may combine assurance with an element of investment gain.

Whole-of-life contracts can be arranged on a number of alternative bases. Traditionally premiums have been reviewable, with the consequence that the premium may be raised to a level where it becomes uneconomic. However, some providers now offer policies whose premium is guaranteed to remain fixed and it may also be possible to arrange a contract where premiums cease at a particular date but the cover continues.

Typically a policy will be arranged on the life of a client and the policy will then be assigned to a trust for the benefit of their intended beneficiaries. So long as the insurance premiums fall within either the annual IHT capital gifts exemptions or the gifts out of income exemption, and provided that the settlor has not reserved an interest in the trust, the sum insured should be paid to the trustees on the death of the insured free of IHT, CGT or IT. This approach can also be used to ensure that sufficient funds are made available to meet a potential IHT charge, so that assets which would otherwise have to be sold to meet the tax bill can be retained by the beneficiaries.

Policies effected in trust before 22 March 2006

In view of the changes to trust taxation which came into effect on Budget Day, 22 March 2006, it is important to review the type of policy used, the form of trust used and the amount of any policy sum assured.

HMRC has confirmed, in relation to policies effected in trust prior to 22 March 2006, that:

- the maintenance of existing premiums paid should not cause the policy to become subject to the IHT provisions which apply to post-21 March 2006 trusts;
- premiums paid should continue to be treated as PETs and should not be CLTs;

- provided that the original policy terms permit, the terms of a policy can be varied post 21 March 2006 without causing the policy to become subject to the new IHT trust provisions. However, it should be noted that if the policy is varied in some way which is not covered by policy options which were available prior to Budget Day 2006, it could become subject to the new IHT provisions;
- any change in named or default beneficiaries which do not qualify under the Transitional Serial Interest or Immediate Post Death Interest rules, would cause the policy to become subject to the new IHT regime.

Policies effected in trust after 21 March 2006

The treatment of arrangements created after 21 March 2006 will depend in part upon the value of the life policy. Most policies have a relatively high sum assured and a relatively low or (in the case of term policies) no surrender value. They should therefore generally have a very low market value until the death of the life assured or until such time as the life assured might become seriously or terminally ill.

IHT charges should not therefore generally arise under most forms of trust unless the sum assured on a policy exceeds the IHT nil rate band allowance and either:

- the settlor is terminally ill at a 10-year anniversary date and is aware of the fact, so that the policy has a market value at this date; or
- death occurs before such an anniversary and the trustees have not distributed the policy proceeds out of the trust at the anniversary date.

In the former situation the trustees could be left in a position where IHT is due but no liquid funds are available to it. For this reason it may be sensible to hold some cash within the trust.

In cases where the sum assured is substantial and/or it is likely that funds will remain in the trust after a claim, it may be appropriate to split the insurance cover into a number of smaller policies at outset, placing each policy in its own trust. So long as each trust is separate it should be entitled to its own IHT nil rate band, thereby reducing the possibility of periodic or exit charges. Where several policies are contemplated it may also be worth spreading the total cover across a number of insurance companies. Most major companies are prepared to co-ordinate underwriting so that, for example, only one medical examination (if any) should be required.

Back-to-back schemes using purchased life annuities

A 'back-to-back' scheme is a combination of a purchased life annuity (PLA), which is purchased with capital, and a life assurance policy (LAP), written under trust (so as to take the sum assured outside the client's estate) and funded by the income derived from the annuity. An element of the income received from the PLA will be deemed for tax purposes to be a return of the capital applied to purchase the annuity and so tax-free. Only the interest element of the income received will be subject to IT, which permits a reasonably tax-efficient income to be derived from these arrangements.

The premiums funded with the capital element of the annuity income will not be eligible for treatment as a gift out of income, but they may fall within the annual exemption for gifts out of capital. If any element of the premiums is not exempt from IHT, the premiums will be treated as CLTs.

This form of planning can be very tax-efficient. The capital applied to purchase the PLA immediately reduces the value of the client's estate as the money has been spent. Effectively, therefore, the loss to the client's heirs is 60 per cent of the purchase price (assuming the capital would have been subject to IHT at 40 per cent if it had remained in the client's estate). That loss is usually more than compensated by the sum assured under the LAP which the heirs will ultimately receive as beneficiaries.

However, caution must be exercised with these arrangements. The recent case of *Smith* v. *HMRC* [2008] WTLR 147 highlights that a back-to-back arrangement can either fall foul of HMRC Statement of Practice E4 or fall to be treated as an associated operation under IHTA 1984, s.268.

In *Smith & Others* the deceased and his wife took out a back-to-back plan under which the first premium on the LAP was paid out of the initial investment and the first annuity payment was used to pay the second premium and so on. At the foot of the illustration was the statement

> Please complete and sign this section if you wish to apply for the policies illustrated . . . you should also complete the relevant proposal form.

The clients completed three application forms, one for each 'combined' plan. Simple application forms comprising six health questions were signed and, at the same time, three trust declarations were signed in respect of 'any with profits endowment assurance'. The provider involved was prepared immediately to issue the wife with the PLA and LAP but requested further medical evidence on the husband. That evidence was received and deemed satisfactory and three PLAs and LAPs were issued, written on a joint life, last survivor basis. The wife died in 2002 and the husband in 2003. HMRC issued notices of determination in 2006 that the vesting of the LAPs on the husband's death constituted a transfer of value by virtue of an associated operation under s.263.

The Special Commissioner considered in detail the three tests of an associated operation laid out in s.268(1)(b) and decided that the arrangement fell foul of the first and third tests (but not the second):

- In relation to the first test, there was sufficient evidence to show that the LAP and the PLA were purchased and made 'with reference to' each other. Although separate policy documents were issued in respect of each, there were sufficient references in the total package of documentation (namely the illustration and the application forms) to justify the conclusion that each pair of PLAs and LAPs formed part of a single contract.
- In relation to the third test, the PLAs were purchased with a view to facilitating the LAPs (this test did not actually require a contractual link and it was sufficient that the receipts from the PLAs made it easier to pay the premiums on the LAPs).

The Special Commissioner also considered HMRC Statement of Practice E4, which states:

> Life assurance policies and annuities are regarded as not being affected by the associated operations rule if first, the policy (i.e. the LAP) was issued on full medical evidence of the life assured's health and second, it would have been issued on the same terms if the annuity had not been bought.

The Special Commissioner found that Statement of Practice E4 did not apply to preclude an associated operation as the provider involved had not sought full medical evidence in relation to the wife, even though the LAPs did not vest on her death (by virtue of their having been arranged on a second death basis). She was still a life assured under the policies.

The Special Commissioner therefore dismissed the taxpayer's appeal and confirmed the Notices of Determination.

On the basis of this decision it should be stressed that:

- it is important that full medical evidence be sought in relation to every life assured under both the PLA and the LPA;
- generally any form of packaged back-to-back arrangement should be avoided and the PLA and the LPA be established as completely separate operations;
- to be safe, it may be appropriate to establish the PLA and the LPA with entirely separate companies and it should be borne in mind that two companies being part of the same group or being linked by a jointly operated reinsurance agreement could increase the risk of an associated operation arising;
- if a client has an existing back-to-back arrangement, this may need to be reviewed in the light of *Smith & Others*.

Equity release and IHT

An equity release scheme could enables a client to mitigate IHT by gifting at least part of the capital tied up in their home whilst at the same time retaining the security of being able to remain in the property for the remainder of their life. The value released would become available as liquid funds available to be spent, gifted directly or applied to an appropriate IHT mitigation arrangement.

As a general rule, it is advisable to regard the home as the last asset to be considered from the point of view of IHT mitigation and, if possible, any action to mitigate liability should be confined to converting or gifting other assets or, if clients are prepared to consider moving to a lower value property, 'down-sizing'. However, these arrangements may be worth considering for clients who:

- own a home worth more than the IHT nil rate band, or double the nil rate band in the case of joint ownership, particularly if the home represents the bulk of their capital;
- do not wish to move home;
- are not concerned about bequeathing the property itself (but are concerned more about maximising the potential amount bequeathed); and
- are prepared to consider selling their home in whole or in part with a view to reducing their IHT liability.

Any privately arranged equity release (e.g. one financed with money raised by other family members) seems likely to be caught either by pre-owned asset tax (POAT) or as a reserved benefit. However, there is a view supported by correspondence with the Capital Taxes Office that it is not HMRC's intention to use POAT legislation to catch commercial, arms' length, equity release transactions.

Pensions

Pensions can provide IHT planning opportunities, some of which are discussed in Chapters 20 and 21.

9

Discounted gift trusts and loan trusts

Richard Hopkins

Beyond the suite of front-line solutions for inheritance tax (IHT) mitigation, including a well-drafted will, the use of annual gift exemptions and simple trusts, there lies a landscape of difficult choices for the average client contemplating estate planning.

Quite often the solution to reducing IHT involves forfeiting access to income and capital and for many clients this may present an insuperable obstacle.

In the financial services world, however, there are proven 'packaged' solutions which can help reduce a client's IHT bill whilst maintaining access to income or capital. These schemes involve the use of the single premium life policy investment vehicle known familiarly as the investment bond.

In this chapter, we focus on the two most well-established investment bond-based solutions, each of which addresses particular client requirements for access to income and/or capital.

Discounted gift trusts

This solution is very much about making both an immediate impact to reduce IHT and then reducing any further liability to zero after seven years – an arrangement which would suit a client who has capital in excess of his or her needs but wishes to retain access to an income stream from that capital.

The scheme is based simply on a gift made by the settlor(s) to a trust set up for one or more beneficiaries. The gift is invested in an investment bond, which is held in a suitable trust arrangement (see below).

When the investment is made, the value of the gift is discounted to reflect the element which is immediately removed from the estate and therefore no longer subject to IHT on death. The balance of the gift will be subject to IHT as a potentially exempt transfer (PET) and will reduce to zero over seven years in accordance with the taper relief rules.

The discount is calculated by the life office within HMRC guidelines, based on the settlor's age, health and the expected period of investment until death. This also takes into account any income withdrawn from the bond by the settlor(s).

This income is normally drawn by the settlor(s) at a rate of 5 per cent of the original sum invested, this being the rate of withdrawal from investment bonds which is regarded by HMRC as a return of capital and therefore not subject to immediate income tax liability. Potential liability to income tax is deferred and is something that the beneficiaries will need to manage at the point they receive the right to access the bond investment upon the death of the settlor(s).

The main disadvantage of the discounted gift trust (DGT) is the loss of access to the capital invested.

> EXAMPLE
>
> If we take a 75-year-old in good health who wants to save IHT on £200,000 of surplus capital, then the following position would be established.
>
> First, an income stream would be agreed for the settlor at the outset. This is typically set at 5 per cent of the capital value as outlined above. So in this example, the settlor now has £10,000 of income per annum.
>
> This income stream will drive the discount, along with age and health (subject to underwriting). If we assume in the example that the discount is 40 per cent, then this means that, in the event of death before the seven years is up (remember the PET rules for a gift), £80,000 will be immediately exempt from the IHT calculation. After seven years the whole of the gift of £200,000 is exempt from IHT, yet the income stream continues.
>
> On death, the beneficiaries will then have access to the proceeds of the trust.

The general IHT position of discounted gift trusts

The effect of the discount as described above will often reduce the value of the transfer below the nil rate band where this has been unused, except in large cases – typically over £500,000. For flexible and discretionary trusts this means no IHT is payable immediately. However, these trusts will be potentially liable to future periodic and exit charges. With regard to absolute trusts, gifts into the trust are still PETs and so there is no immediate charge anyway. However, the discount will become relevant should the PET become chargeable on the death of the settlor within seven years.

In situations where, even with a discount, the value of a chargeable transfer is still above the nil rate band, it is still possible to avoid initial IHT charges. By splitting the investment into two trusts, one absolute (or 'bare') trust and one flexible or discretionary trust, the chargeable transfer can be kept below the available nil rate band and an immediate IHT charge can be avoided.

Payment of capital made from a flexible or a discretionary trust may, however, be subject to an 'exit' charge. As exit charges are based on the last periodic charge, the lower the periodic charge, the lower the exit charge. Splitting the investment between flexible or discretionary trusts and absolute trusts and creating the flexible or discretionary trust first will help to achieve this.

Loan trusts

As with the DGT, a loan trust is based on a single premium investment bond which is held within a suitable trust arrangement. It differs from a DGT in that the principal capital is not gifted and therefore no discount is available for tax purposes. Instead, a loan is made to the trust for the benefit of the nominated beneficiaries, the trust having been established with a gift of nominal value, such as £10.

The loan funds are invested to achieve capital growth, and whatever growth is achieved is immediately free of IHT, as it forms part of the trust. The original capital, however, remains subject in full to IHT, as it is merely a loan to the trust and is only reduced by the amount of the repayments which are made to the settlor(s). These loan repayments are interest-free and as the arrangement is fixed within an investment bond structure, the settlor will normally withdraw up to 5 per cent of the original capital invested, to provide a tax-deferred income.

This type of arrangement best suits a client who is looking to retain access to his or her capital and to continue to receive income from the funds. The IHT savings are not as generous as the DGT and derive mainly from the investment growth which may hopefully be achieved over longer periods of time. As long as the repayments are spent by the settlor, the loan and therefore the capital will have been fully repaid and depleted after 20 years, whilst the growth on the capital would be held in the trust free of IHT.

There is in fact one version of this structure which also adds the loan repayments to the trust value on death, thus preserving both the principal capital and growth for the beneficiaries over the 20 years.

The following example shows how the scheme operates using an investment bond. It is not necessary to link the scheme directly to investment markets and it can be effected on a guaranteed or a deposit basis, where the return is directly linked to interest rates, or on a 'with profits' basis with annual bonuses.

EXAMPLE

Loan trust set up for		£100,000
Trustees repay 5% p.a. as tax-free 'income' loan repayment		£ 5,000

Assuming the investment bond increases in value by 7 per cent per annum net of charges, but including re-investments of income:

IHT position after:	5 Years	10 Years	15 Years
Trust value	£111,500	£127,630	£150,250
Remaining loan	£ 75,000	£ 50,000	£ 25,000
Balance free of IHT (trust value less loan)	£ 36,500	£ 77,630	£125,250
Tax saved at 40%	£ 14,600	£ 31,052	£ 50,100

This example is for illustrative purposes only.

Loan trusts and the 10-year periodic charge and exit charge

Even though the loan trust does not result in an immediate charge to IHT, an IIP trust (the flexible trust under the loan trust) has been created and is a settlement for the purposes of the Inheritance Tax Act 1984, s.43. Under the Finance Act 2006 this means that the loan trust is subject to the periodic and exit charges, where applicable.

Every 10 years, the trust will be subject to a 'periodic charge'. Where the settlor has not made any chargeable lifetime transfers (CLTs) in the seven years before they set up the plan, and the value of the trust fund on the periodic charge date is less than the nil-rate band at that time, there will be no tax to be paid.

If any payments are made out of the trust to the beneficiaries (that is, any growth in the value of the bond excluding the outstanding loan) then any exit charge tax payable is based on the tax charge at the last periodic charge date. Therefore, if the tax charge at the last periodic charge date was zero then the exit charge will be zero. If there was a tax charge at the last periodic charge date, then the exit charge will be based on this. If a payment is made before the first periodic charge date then any exit charge will be based on the tax when the original gift was made into the trust. Repayments of the loan to the settlor are not treated as 'exits'.

Trusts and taxation issues

Prior to the Finance Act 2006, many of the above schemes used flexible power of appointment trusts with an interest in possession (IIP), so-called 'flexible trusts'. The advantage was that the gift into this type of trust was a potentially exempt transfer and so would not result in an immediate IHT charge, irrespective of the size of the gift into trust.

This all changed after the Finance Act 2006 came into force. Flexible trusts no longer offer this benefit, and gifts into such trusts on or after 22 March 2006 are now treated in the same way as gifts into discretionary trusts; that is to say, they are deemed chargeable transfers. This means that if the gift, when added to any other chargeable transfers made in the seven years prior to the gift, exceeds the IHT nil rate band (£312,000 in 2008/09), there will be an immediate IHT charge on the excess at the lifetime rate of 20 per cent.

Flexible trusts and discretionary trusts may also suffer IHT charges on the trust itself every 10 years, or whenever capital is distributed to a beneficiary. It is worth noting, however, that absolute trusts do not suffer these ongoing charges and some modern plans are set up on this basis.

Other points to note

Both of the above schemes are available within onshore and offshore investment bond structures and as such are taxed differently. The gross roll-up tax advantage of offshore investment bonds over onshore bonds will counter the higher costs of the offshore bond wrapper over the longer term. However, the tax status of the beneficiaries will need to be taken into account.

In many cases, the beneficiaries are the children. At the point that they look to encash the bond on the death of the settlor(s), income tax is potentially payable by the beneficiary depending on their personal tax status, and so careful planning is required for this to be mitigated. For a typical UK resident and domiciled beneficiary, offshore bonds are subject to the full income tax charge of up to 40 per cent. However, within an onshore bond this may result in no further liability to income tax should the beneficiary's income plus gain fall below the higher rate tax threshold, as basic rate tax will have been accounted for within the bond.

Finally, it is important to ensure that the strategy adopted for the investment of funds within the bond is appropriate to the achievement of investment growth sufficient both to accommodate settlors' withdrawals and also to preserve the value of the fund against inflation and charges for the benefit of the ultimate beneficiaries.

10

Tax planning for the expatriate

Jeremy Davis

Emigration

Figures from the Office for National Statistics show that record numbers of people are leaving Britain every year. Over the last 10 years, 1.6 million Britons have emigrated. Of those who left in 2006, nearly 30 per cent went to live in Australia or New Zealand and 25 per cent went to live in Spain or France. There has been substantial immigration over the same period.

The main focus of this section is on Europe, and Spain and France in particular, these being the most popular havens for UK nationals. Tax regimes clearly differ, but there are some general principles which this section will endeavour to highlight.

Among the matters to be considered when moving abroad is the timing of becoming non-resident for UK tax purposes. It may be possible to take a tax holiday for a few months while establishing residence in the new country. If it looks likely that an offshore trust will be advisable, then this should be established before becoming resident in the new country.

If the person is staying abroad for at least five years, it may be possible to sell UK property without incurring UK capital gains tax (CGT). The inheritance tax (IHT) laws in the country of destination will almost certainly be different from those in the UK, and estate planning will need to take into account the UK tax laws as well as the new country's laws on inheritance. This will almost certainly mean making a will in the new country.

Mortgages may be tax-deductible in the country of destination, as it is in the UK for rental income. However, having a mortgage on the house may reduce its value for local succession taxes.

There may also be wealth tax in the country of destination and it is important to understand the local income taxes and any double taxation agreement with the UK. In terms of day-to-day living, expatriates may find the tax rates higher in Spain than in the UK. For example, Spanish income tax starts at 24 per cent and rises to 43 per cent; and unlike the tax regime in the UK, there are two other tax bands in between.

For people retiring abroad, it is important to consider the payment of pensions, and the way these are taxed in the country of destination. In

Spain, the taxation of pension annuities is more favourable than in the UK, because the capital return element is not taxed.

Becoming non-resident

Normally, a tax year is taken as a whole when determining tax residence status, but a tax year can be split in certain circumstances. If an individual leaves the UK to live abroad for a period of at least three years, he or she will be treated as non-resident from the day of departure. Similarly, if they leave to take up full-time employment for at least one year, they will be treated as non-resident from the day of departure.

This can create the opportunity for a tax holiday, when the individual is not resident anywhere for tax purposes. For example, the tax year in Spain runs from 1 January to 31 December, and so anyone moving there in the second half of the year will not become tax-resident until the following year. This can provide an opportunity to arrange affairs in a more tax-efficient manner, for example using an offshore trust.

To remain non-resident and not ordinarily resident in the UK, the following conditions must be met:

- you must spend less than 183 days in the UK each year, including arrival and departure days;
- you must have spent, on average, fewer than 91 days per tax year in the UK over the past four years.

Provided these conditions are met, there will be no CGT on disposals in the UK, no UK tax on FOTRA (Free of Tax for Residents Abroad) securities (e.g. Gilts), and a claim can be made using form R105 for interest from building societies and banks to be paid free of tax. If there is earned income in the UK, normal tax allowances can be claimed.

Retiring abroad

The UK state pension is paid gross, but may be taxable in the country of residence. Income from occupational and personal pensions is normally taxed in the UK under PAYE unless a claim is made for it to be paid gross. There are HMRC forms for individual countries, for example FD5 for France and FD9 for Spain, which need to be filed with the local tax authorities. Completing the form ensures that the pension is taxable in the country of residence, and permits the reimbursement of any UK tax that may have been paid while the form was being filed. UK government service pensions (civil service, local authority, armed forces, police, fire, teachers) are taxed in the UK, but may be taken into account in the country of residence for determining the effective rate of tax payable on other income.

When taking the benefits from a pension, it is important to establish whether or not any tax-free lump sum will be regarded as tax free in the country of residence. In France, it is normally treated as tax free, but in Spain it may be taxable. There is also some confusion about how pension annuities should be taxed, because in some countries (e.g. Spain) there is not a clear distinction between a purchased life annuity and a pension annuity.

Pensions can be transferred abroad, provided the receiving scheme is registered with HMRC as a qualifying recognised overseas pension scheme (QROPS). Most UK pension schemes, including those in drawdown, can be transferred to a QROPS, including 'protected rights' accrued from con-tracted-out contributions. The exceptions are the state pension and most final salary schemes which are in payment. The trustees of a QROPS are obliged to report any 'benefit crystallisation event' to HMRC during the first five years of non-UK tax residence. Once this period has elapsed, there is no requirement for the trustees to report to HMRC. The typical features are:

- distributions can only be made on retirement, death or total permanent incapacity;
- distributions can be a maximum of 30 per cent cash, with the balance being applied to provide an income for life;
- there is no requirement for a QROPS to purchase an annuity or 'alternatively secured pension' (ASP) at age 75 (see Chapter 20);
- QROPS are potentially suitable for those who have already emigrated from the UK on a permanent basis, non-domiciles who will return home, and those intending to emigrate from the UK on a permanent basis in the near future;
- QROPS are not suitable for those who remain domiciled and tax-resident in the UK or those who intend to return to the UK on a permanent basis.

Buying property abroad

If the property is going to be let, it is probably better to get a local mort-gage where possible in order to benefit from any tax relief. Mortgages in Spain are usually for a maximum term of 15 years, and on a repayment basis. Having a mortgage reduces the net value of the property, which can have the effect of reducing any liability to local IHT. In later life, equity release plans can be used for the same purpose.

It is important to establish fully the costs of buying, which may be considerably more than in the UK, and to understand the local property tax system. As well as Notary's fees and land registration fees, in Spain there is a tax payable on the transfer of value between private individuals, known as *impuesto sobre transmisiones patrimoniales* (ITP). There is also stamp duty known as *impuesto sobre actos juridicos documentados* (AJD) to pay. It is very important to seek legal advice.

Most people will be buying a second home or a retirement home in their own names, but some may be buying property abroad as an investment using a corporate structure. The tax implications of this will need to be assessed, and legal advice sought.

It is important to assess the implications of owning a property abroad on IHT and succession taxes. To avoid French succession tax between spouses, for example, it may be advisable to buy the property in joint names, and execute a French community marriage contract (*communauté universelle*). This means that the surviving spouse inherits the jointly owned assets, and the asset does not have to pass to the children. This type of arrangement does not work, however, if there is a child from a previous marriage.

Care needs to be taken when using a corporate structure, for example a *société civile immobilière* (SCI) in France, because the benefit in kind of providing accommodation may be taxable in the UK. The reason the SCI approach has been commonly used by non-French residents is that the French succession laws do not apply to the shares of an SCI, though succession tax may still be payable.

Wealth tax is payable in France on net assets greater than €760,000, but no longer in Spain.

Income and capital gains taxes

Once individuals become tax-resident in Spain, they are taxable on their worldwide assets. This is different from the position in the UK, where the domicile rules apply. The disposal of a UK property by an individual who is not resident and not ordinarily resident will normally be exempt from CGT in the UK, but there will be a liability to Spanish CGT for those who are tax-resident there, and otherwise it will be necessary to check the local tax laws.

Capital gains are taxed at a single rate of 18 per cent in Spain, the same as in the UK, but there is no annual exemption. Nor is taper relief available any longer, other than for shares bought before 1995. Realised gains on property can be carried forward to a new property by residents in Spain, and the same applies to investment funds. Those aged over 65 who are tax resident in Spain are not liable for capital gains on property.

Income tax, *impuesto sobre la renta de las personas físicas* (IRPF) in Spain is subject to a personal allowance of €5,050, and €900 extra for those over 65. The tax rate percentage goes in steps from 24 to 28, 37 and 43 per cent, so it can be more onerous than in the UK, although pension annuities are taxed more favourably.

Savings income such as interest, dividends and proceeds from life assurance contracts are taxed at a fixed rate of 18 per cent. It is no longer possible to claim back the 10 per cent tax credit on UK dividends in Spain, but to compensate for this there is an exemption of 1,500 on dividends (only shares, not collective investments).

Wealth tax in Spain or *impuesto sobre el patrimonio* (IP) was abolished during 2008, and backdated from 1 January 2008, as part of a number of measures to provide a fiscal stimulus to the flagging economy. Wealth tax is, however, still a feature of the French tax system.

Inheritance tax

A UK-domiciled non-resident is liable for IHT on their worldwide assets. In Spain, for example, a non-Spanish resident in Spain is liable for their equivalent succession tax, *impuesto de sucesiones y donaciones* (ISD) also on their worldwide assets, so there is scope for double taxation, although the Spanish tax authorities will take into account any UK tax paid. The top rate of tax for ISD is 81.6 per cent, compared with 40 per cent for IHT in the UK. Clearly, this would be a major consideration for people retiring abroad.

IHT may work differently outside the UK. Again, taking the example of Spain, the tax is levied on the beneficiary, not the estate. If the beneficiaries are not resident in Spain, they will be liable for ISD on the assets they inherit that are in Spain, but they will not be liable for assets elsewhere, which may be subject to IHT on the estate.

Exemptions and reliefs in Spain vary from one region to another. The residence status of the deceased determines whether the Spanish national tax rules apply, or the regional variation, because it is necessary to be habitually resident in the region for five years to benefit from local rules. Unlike the position in the UK regime, ISD is potentially payable on first death between spouses. Some regions in Spain (e.g. Valencia) have acted to reduce considerably the impact of ISD, particularly between spouses.

It is important to note that the tax rate between spouses is much more favourable than between unmarried partners. Because the tax is on the beneficiary, there are different tax rates according to how closely related the beneficiary is to the deceased, with more distant relatives or trustees being taxed more harshly. For this reason, it is not generally a good idea for assets to pass via a will to a trust. There are complicated personal allowances, equivalent to the nil rate band, which depend on the closeness of the relationship between the deceased and the beneficiaries.

There is a relief for inheriting a main residence in Spain (for which there is no equivalent in the UK); and business property relief is available at 95 per cent, provided the business is kept going for five years after death (compared to 100 per cent in the UK).

Inheritance itself may work differently from the UK, so it is important to have a will for the new country of residence.

Life insurance payouts are taxed in Spain, with small personal allowances, so placing a whole-of-life insurance policy in trust, which is popular in the UK, does not work in Spain.

Gifts in Spain cumulate over three years (compared to seven years in the UK) for the purposes of determining the applicable tax rate, but there are generally no personal allowances applicable to gifts (though practice varies from one region to another).

For beneficiaries not resident in Spain, one approach to mitigating ISD that has been popular is equity release, taking the cash released offshore, thereby reducing the net assets liable to ISD, and permitting tax planning for IHT using trusts.

IHT is clearly a very complex area of interaction between UK and local tax laws, with a great deal of scope for planning, but requiring specialist knowledge of the country in question.

11

Investment strategies for non-UK domiciled but resident individuals

Paul Garwood

Before 6 April 2008

The rules governing the taxation of UK resident but non-UK domiciled individuals, i.e. those whose country of closest attachment is outside the UK, were changed significantly as of 6 April 2008.

Prior to this, such individuals were able avoid tax on their overseas investment income, capital gains and earnings to the extent that these were not remitted to the UK.

Furthermore, they could remit income from sources which had ceased in a prior fiscal year and establish offshore trusts which provided them with full protection from capital gains tax (CGT) on sales of assets whether these were UK or overseas sited.

It was also possible for gifts representing offshore income and capital gains to be made to close relatives who could then bring them into the UK without crystallising a tax charge, provided that the transferor did not benefit.

Mindful that many such individuals were able to avoid UK tax relatively easily, HMRC introduced rule changes to restrict future planning opportunities.

This section, whilst not providing a full technical appraisal of the changes, will highlight the fact that despite the new rules such individuals can still reduce UK tax on income and gains arising on their overseas assets with careful investment-based planning.

The new rules

Whilst the remittance basis will remain, non-UK domiciled individuals who have been resident in the UK in at least seven of the previous nine fiscal years will now have to pay a remittance basis charge of £30,000 per annum as well as losing their UK personal income tax and CGT allowances. If they do not make the claim and pay this charge they will be assessed to tax on their worldwide income as it arises in the same way as UK domiciled individuals (the 'arising basis').

Non-UK domiciled but resident individuals who have not been resident in the UK for at least seven out of the previous nine fiscal years can remain on the remittance basis and will not have to pay the remittance basis charge, but will lose their tax allowances.

The source ceasing rules have also been abolished which effectively means that it will not be possible to remit any offshore income without it being taxed. This will apply to all overseas income, whether it arose before or after the changes, unless it had previously been remitted.

The other key change is that certain offshore trusts established by non-domiciled settlors will cease to be wholly exempt from UK CGT although the remittance basis will apply to gains on overseas assets.

Finally, the alienation of offshore income and capital gains to spouses, civil partners, or anyone living with someone in these capacities, minor children and grandchildren, will bring them into charge to tax if they are subsequently brought into the UK. Interestingly, these new rules do not apply to some income which arose before 6 April 2008.

The problems

In the past, non-UK domiciled individuals would have been able to separate their untainted overseas capital from income arising to it as well as avoiding CGT on any investment growth. This enabled them to remit both capital and capital gains without suffering a UK tax liability. Furthermore, provided they waited until the year after the source of the income had ceased, they could then remit it to the UK without charge.

Using offshore trusts to realise tax-free capital gains which can be remitted will no longer be possible. Furthermore, it will not generally be possible to remit the income without it being taxed.

Investors and advisers therefore need to consider ways that 'clean' capital can be invested in future, so that capital, income and capital gains can continue to be segregated and tax-efficient remittances made.

They will also want to consider whether they can avoid the £30,000 tax charge and minimise tax on income and gains arising on their offshore assets.

Individual circumstances

Personal circumstances will differ and it is vital for advisers to have a complete understanding of their clients' overall position. They will first need to establish whether the individual is in fact not domiciled in the UK. HMRC is now looking more closely at the circumstances surrounding an individuals' claims for non-domiciled status and the level of their scrutiny can be expected to increase.

It will also become more relevant to determine when an individual becomes resident in the UK for at least seven of the past nine years and to look very carefully at the constituent parts of their overseas capital and cash funds.

Finally, estimating the quantum of clients' overseas income will also be important so that a comparison can be made between the tax payable on an arising basis and the £30,000 remittance basis charge and the loss of personal income and CGT allowances.

Individuals need to be generating at least £85,000 of offshore income before it becomes beneficial for them to pay the remittance basis charge. Assuming investment returns of between 3 and 5 per cent, those with offshore capital of between £1.7m and £2.8m are likely to be on the cusp of the remittance basis charge and will require most thought to be given to their affairs.

It is also fair to assume that anyone who has been in the UK for more than seven out of the previous nine years will want to maintain the status quo as far as possible.

With this in mind, any investment vehicle which rolls up income and capital gains and permits the investor both to avoid the £30,000 remittance basis charge and to avoid or defer tax on income and gains arising each year is likely to be attractive.

The solutions

First, will it be possible in future to segregate capital, capital gains and income? Whilst most investments segregate income from capital they do not segregate capital from capital gains.

There are, however, investments that roll up income and capital without giving rise to a tax liability until they are disposed of. These are divided into those that roll up income and capital gains without segregating these from the original capital, and those that roll up income and capital gains whilst enabling the investor to segregate this from the original capital invested.

The former will enable individuals to avoid the £30,000 tax charge, assuming they elect to be taxed on the arising basis, and to minimise their tax liabilities, whilst the latter will offer the greater scope for financial planning.

How are traditional offshore investments affected?

Offshore bank deposits

It is possible to segregate deposit interest from capital, thus enabling individuals on the remittance basis to remit 'clean' capital. Individuals who have been resident for seven out of the previous nine years will either have to pay tax on the interest arising or pay the £30,000 remittance basis charge. Furthermore, if they have currency deposits they will need to be mindful of currency gains when switches are made into Sterling.

Stocks, shares, OEICs, SICAVs and UCITs

It is possible to segregate dividends and interest from capital in these traditional 'long only' (i.e. not employing 'shorting' techniques) investment vehicles, but capital gains cannot be segregated from the original capital. Owners of these investments will not be able to remit the capital or dividends to the UK without suffering a tax charge. Those who have been resident for seven out of the previous nine years will be subject to the £30,000 remittance basis charge unless they pay tax on their dividends on the arising basis.

They will therefore need to balance the £30,000 remittance basis charge and the loss of personal UK tax allowances against tax that would otherwise be payable on an arising basis on these investments.

Offshore non-distributor status funds (e.g. hedge funds and property funds)

Such investments, as implied by their name, roll up income and gains. However, the gains arising on the disposal of these assets will be subject to income tax if remitted, or on the arising basis.

Assuming investors do not dispose of these investments until such time as they are not liable to UK tax, e.g. after they have ceased to be UK resident, they can avoid the £30,000 remittance basis charge and retain their personal income and CGT allowances while the investments roll up offshore.

It should be noted, however, that whilst individuals can control their tax liabilities in this way there may be overriding investment considerations which mean that a disposal of the asset becomes necessary for reasons not related to tax. This does therefore create some uncertainty.

Offshore investment bonds

These investment vehicles may fulfil all of the needs of the non-UK domiciled investor as they have their own unique tax treatment which can fit in well with many of the scenarios envisaged above.

Legal structure

These investments are non-qualifying policies of insurance provided by offshore insurance companies based notably in the Isle of Man, Channel Islands, Luxembourg and other offshore financial centres.

Whilst they are, effectively, collective investment vehicles they have certain advantages over other collectives as they have their own unique tax treatment.

It is this tax treatment which makes offshore bonds attractive to both UK domiciled and non-UK domiciled investors, although the advantages to the latter group have grown significantly in importance since the changes in the rules governing the taxation of non-domiciled individuals as of 6 April 2008.

Taxation

The tax rules which apply to offshore bonds are as follows:

- An offshore bond is considered to be a non-income-producing asset.
- Income and gains can roll up 'tax free' within the bond, subject to irrecoverable withholding taxes on dividends.
- Investment switches within the bond can be made without triggering tax liabilities at the time. This gives investment flexibility which is completely free of tax constraints.
- Withdrawals of up to 5 per cent of the original capital invested can be made annually without giving rise to a tax liability on accrued income and gains within the bond. To the extent that this allowance is not used in any one year, it can be carried forward to the next and subsequent years.
- Unlike investments which are subject to CGT, offshore bonds can be assigned from one person to another without giving rise to a tax liability on any underlying income and gains.
- Income and gains are subject to UK income tax at the UK resident investor's highest marginal rate when withdrawals in excess of the 5 per cent allowance are made by way of partial surrender, or on full surrender, or on the death of the last of the lives assured under the contract.
- Income tax is payable on any gain at up to 40 per cent, rising to 45 per cent for some individuals as of 2011/12, as opposed to an 18 per cent

CGT charge. Depending again on the individual's circumstances both now and in the future this is another factor which must be considered carefully when planning.

- Top slicing relief may be available which can in some circumstances and with careful planning reduce the overall tax on any gain.

Planning for non-UK domiciled individuals

The foregoing rules can, in some circumstances, be extremely tax-efficient for non-domiciled individuals for the following reasons:

- Individuals with clean capital can invest in a bond and then withdraw up to 5 per cent of the original amount invested each year which they can then use to fund their living in the UK. This will enable them to both avoid the £30,000 remittance basis charge and tax on an arising basis.
- Individuals who have capital which is 'tainted' with income can also invest in such bonds. Whilst the 5 per cent withdrawals cannot be used to fund their expenditure in the UK, it can be used to fund overseas expenditure. Again, such individuals who have been resident for at least seven out of the previous nine years can avoid the £30,000 remittance basis charge as well as tax on an arising basis.
- Individuals who have not been resident for seven out of the previous nine years and who want investment flexibility might invest in these vehicles in anticipation of that date approaching. In due course this would enable them to utilise the 5 per cent allowances in the same way as referred to above.
- Assuming that the non-UK domiciled individual returns to his or her country of origin or leaves the UK to live elsewhere, they will be able to encash the bond either in part or in full once they have departed. This should enable them to avoid UK taxes, although they will need to explore their tax position in their then country of residence. As part of any initial planning process, it is strongly recommended that the taxation of offshore bonds in their ultimate jurisdiction of encashment is considered. Furthermore, some jurisdictions do not recognise offshore bonds as insurance policies and this must also be taken into account.
- It is possible to assign the offshore bond to someone who is not liable to UK tax, who can then encash it.

Other matters

As offshore bonds are insurance policies, there will always be an element of life cover, usually equivalent to 1 per cent of the total fund value. Furthermore, as an encashment occurs on the death of the last of the lives assured under the policy it is usual for provision to be made for multiple lives assured. This should ensure that there are no unintended encashments which might lead to unwanted income tax liabilities.

US taxpayers need to be mindful that offshore bond providers do not allow them to invest.

Investments in offshore bonds

Offshore bonds can invest in all asset classes and investment sectors although only through collective funds. They can also invest in cash deposits.

Some investors can establish their own collective vehicles which, in turn, can hold single stocks and shares although generally the minimum required investment would be £5m.

Switches between the collective funds and/or the single stocks and shares held within a personalised collective are not subject to CGT. As previously mentioned, this allows investment managers much more scope to make investment decisions uninhibited by tax constraints.

Costs

Many people assume that offshore bonds are expensive investment wrappers. However, the fact is that they are a wrapper similar to a self-invested personal pension (SIPP) and with similar charges. There is, however, a wide range of offshore bond providers with different charging structures, service standards and investment options, and some providers are noticeably more expensive than others, so it is important to compare charges.

The managers of the underlying collective funds will have their own annual management charge which can vary between 0.5 and 2.5 per cent, depending on the type of fund, but the offshore bond provider will be responsible for investment administration and dealing and their charges will generally be either a fixed percentage of the funds or an annual fee. Some providers charge dealing fees separately on a per transaction basis although these may be discounted, depending on transaction numbers.

Advisers will charge for establishing an offshore bond, and some establishment charges are deducted at the outset so that the underlying investment is reduced immediately whilst others take the charge from the fund over a period of five years by way of increased annual fees. In the latter case there will be penalties if the bond is encashed during this initial five-year period. It should be noted that if the establishment fees are paid out of the investment they will be regarded as forming part of its base cost. Furthermore, no VAT is generally payable on fees for setting up these contracts as they are packaged products.

Finally, it should be noted that offshore bonds will enable investors to reduce their personal investment administration costs as the administration of the bond and the investments within it are undertaken by the bond provider. Furthermore, as they are non-income producing assets, income and gains within the bond do not have to be entered on annual tax returns unless there is a partial or full surrender or on death. Providers will report chargeable events to HMRC and will also send valuations to investors when requested. These cost savings are not always considered by investors and can be quite significant, particularly within trusts where there is a requirement to produce annual accounts.

Trusts

12

Principles of portfolio construction

Noel Farrelly

Solicitors, in the course of their daily lives, will often be involved in situations where large lump sums change hands. These events may include the establishment of a trust, a business sale, receipt of an inheritance or a divorce settlement. For the client involved this may be the first time they have had to deal with the investment of such a sum and they may well seek guidance on what they should expect from an investment adviser in these circumstances. Equally, solicitors may be approached for their views on existing investment portfolios or may have responsibilities as trustees. This summary of the portfolio construction process may assist solicitors in these circumstances.

Factfinding

It almost goes without saying that comprehensive information should be gathered by the investment adviser, to include the client's current situation, assets, liabilities, income, future income requirements, objectives, important relationships, investment experience and values. Given the growing interest in 'socially responsible' investing, time should also be taken to elicit the client's views in the areas of ethical and environmentally friendly investments.

A vital component of the initial part of the process will be to establish the client's tolerance of and capacity for risk. Fortunately, we have moved on from the days when the client was expected to characterise his or her attitude to risk as 'high, medium or low'. More sophisticated approaches are now used, including psychometric questionnaires which enable advisers to rate clients against many thousands of others and place them on a normal distribution curve in relation to their appetite for risk.

An alternative approach is to allocate a risk rating to each of the various potential components of a portfolio and, when a possible portfolio has been assembled, to use a simple program to calculate the average weighted risk of the portfolio, reflecting the sums allocated to each component. Advocates of this system contend that it assists in educating clients in the principle of relative risk and the benefits of diversification. Whatever system might be used, it is important that a reasoned approach is seen to have been adopted.

Additional information as to the client's capacity for risk can be gleaned from their other investment holdings and sources of income. A client with large investment holdings elsewhere or reliable and/or growing sources of income may be prepared to take more risk than the client whose only capital is that currently under discussion. Equally, clients may feel less cautious about their non-pension investments than their pension savings. It is also important to realise that tolerance of and capacity for risk may change over the years and the adviser should make clear the need to keep these aspects of the client situation under review.

Asset allocation

The next step in the process is asset allocation. A seminal study by Brinson, Hood and Beebower in 1986, 'Determinants of portfolio performance', published in *Financial Analysts Journal*, concluded that more than 90 per cent of the variability of portfolio returns can be explained by asset allocation, whereas stock selection and market timing accounted for virtually nothing.

The study concentrated on stocks, fixed interest securities and cash, and many portfolio managers will utilise only these asset classes with the possible addition of commercial property. Asset allocation itself is largely driven by the principles of the modern portfolio theory, at the heart of which is diversification, further refined by the desirability of ensuring that the various portfolio components will not all move in the same direction in response to changing market conditions – a concept known as non-correlation.

Many managers will argue that a greater number of asset classes are now available, including, among others, commodities, private equity and structured products. However, there is some dispute in the investment world as to whether these new asset classes offer additional returns and a lack of correlation.

At this point there should also be a discussion about income requirements and the liquidity or otherwise of certain assets. Stocks and bonds can be traded freely on recognised exchanges, but the same does not necessarily apply to commercial property and structured products, as has been demonstrated in recent times.

Selecting funds

The adviser's next step should be to recommend suitable funds or securities within each of the selected asset classes. Some prefer to use a passive approach, others an active approach and some adopt a blended strategy, with passive funds at the core and active funds or managers selected to provide exposure to particular areas. It will be up to the adviser to agree with the investor which approach should be adopted.

The rationale for the selection of funds will be based on track record, the strategy and investment philosophy of the manager, the way in which holdings complement each other and, finally, cost.

Some advisers advocate a discretionary service in preference to an advisory service: the former giving authority to the adviser to buy and sell funds or securities and make changes to the portfolio without prior reference to the client. By contrast, an advisory service requires the client to sign off any changes recommended by the adviser. Many discretionary managers will argue that discretion is required in order that they can act quickly on the client's behalf without seeking authority. The decision may turn on the extent to which the client wishes to be involved in the investment process.

Once the portfolio has been constructed, the portfolio characteristics should be explained to the investor. These will consist of the expected return from the portfolio, together with its volatility. The expected return and volatility will necessarily be based upon historical data, usually over the longest possible time period. The forecast return, although hypothetical, might suitably be based on the capital asset pricing model which forms part of modern portfolio theory. This allows the adviser to indicate a range of returns and the associated volatility from the recommended portfolio, based on past performance. The adviser should, however, make it clear to the client that this should not be treated as a prediction and that short-term volatility in particular can exceed the given range.

Discussion of the characteristics of a proposed portfolio may lead to modifications of the proposals, until the client is happy that the required balance has been achieved between his or her objectives and the level of risk which he or she is willing to tolerate in a worst-case scenario. There should be probing questioning of the client on this point, as intellectually accepting a relatively large drop in portfolio value is never the same as actually experiencing it.

Tax considerations

Tax will be an important consideration for every investor and the next part of the process will be to recommend suitable tax-wrappers for the selected investments. There are a number to choose from and the suitability of each wrapper depends entirely on individual circumstances. Crucial to this is the client's current tax position and likely future tax position, and the client must be asked to share future plans with the adviser so as to ensure that no mistakes are made at this point that would be expensive to repair later.

The rise of online portfolio dealing and management platforms, known as 'wrap' platforms, has made portfolio construction and administration simpler for both client and adviser and such platforms enable the adviser to access all of the main tax-wrappers, such as pensions, individual savings accounts, insurance bonds and investment portfolio accounts electronically. Using a wrap enables the adviser to avoid the complications of needing to choose different providers for each wrapper. Reporting to the client is also much simpler and in most cases clients can be provided with electronic access to their portfolios via the internet. In addition, on the more progressive wrap platforms, switches and rebalancing can be undertaken quickly and easily and at low, or in some cases nil, cost. If the client intends to draw an income, this will be taken into account at this point.

Portfolio reviews

It is important that clients should be reminded in both good times and bad of the risks they are running, and the investment adviser's process should include periodic reviews, when up-dated values can be reported and progress discussed.

This whole process should be documented and the final document will become the client's investment policy statement or investment plan. It should be a clear and cogent explanation of the entire procedure and will remain the basis for investing for the client until it is reviewed, which should be at least once per year. Each time changes are made a new document should be produced, providing an audit trail of changing attitudes, portfolio components, objectives and circumstances.

13

The impact of tax on trustee investment

Ian Muirhead

The Standard Investment Criteria

The Trustee Act 2000, s.3 permits a trustee to: 'make any kind of investment that he could make if he were absolutely entitled to the assets of the
trust', but this general power is subject to s.4 of the Act, which requires
trustees, when exercising their investment powers, to have regard to
'standard investment criteria', which are defined as:

(a)   the suitability to the trust of investments . . . and
(b)   the need for diversification . . .

At the time when the Act was drafted it might have been assumed that the
requirement for suitability and diversification would be satisfied by a then
typical stockbroker portfolio comprising a 20 per cent allocation to gilts,
with the balance in FTSE 100 stocks and perhaps some smaller companies.
However, times have changed, and as discretionary manager Rensburg
commented in the July 2008 edition of the Citywire magazine:

> The key change to take place in recent years is a move towards using fewer
> direct equity holdings and more collectives. With the world as it is now, we
> could not hope to provide proper diversification by just going down the direct
> route.

The current consensus of opinion is that effective diversification should
involve a range of investment building blocks, including property, commodities, hedge funds and alternative investments. However, with the
increased globalisation of industries and the convergence of economies,
the world's major stock markets tend now to move increasingly in unison;
and at times of extreme global tension even those markets which have in
the past been regarded as suitable diversifiers from the standard equity/
bond proposition, such as the emerging markets, property and commodities, have been sucked into the vortex, leaving a simple choice between
risky investment-based asset classes on the one hand and cash or near-cash

on the other, principally in the form of secure government paper (though some have questioned even the government's ability to pay its debts).

Investment 'tax-wrappers'

The suitability of investment recommendations encompasses diversification, but it extends to other considerations, notably the trade-off between risk and return, time span and the sophistication of the client. Also important are the tax efficiency of the arrangements and the desirability of minimising administrative expenses, and it is in this context that the question arises of selecting the most suitable 'tax-wrappers', or investment vehicles, through which the investments are to be held.

The main choice here is between, on the one hand, the unit trust, its EU counterpart the open-ended investment company (OEIC) and its closed-ended counterpart the investment trust; and on the other hand the single premium life insurance policy, or investment bond. Each of these types of vehicle has different tax treatment, and this must be related to the tax treatment of the two main types of trust.

Unit trusts, OEICs and investment trusts are subject to corporation tax at 20 per cent on their taxable income, but are exempt from tax on their capital gains. In practice they pay little or no tax, the principle being that income and gains pass through to the investor. The result is the same as if the investor had invested directly in the underlying securities in the fund. In the case of equity funds, income available for distribution is taxed as company dividends on investors, whether it is distributed or accumulated within the fund. In the case of fixed interest funds, distributions of interest can be made instead of dividends, so investors are deemed to receive interest under deduction of tax at the savings rate.

Investment bonds permit access to similar ranges of funds, but being insurance policies they produce no income for the investor. Whatever income arises within the fund is reinvested to increase the overall return; and investments within the fund enjoy particularly favourable tax treatment. Within an investment bond, savings income is taxed at 20 per cent and dividend income is subject to no further taxation as the 10 per cent tax credit satisfies the life fund's liability to corporation tax. So investment bonds provide an effective means for those who pay tax at a higher rate than the standard rate, including trustees, to defer tax liability and roll up investment returns.

Another major advantage of investment bonds is that investors are entitled to withdraw 5 per cent of the original investment value each year for 20 years to provide an 'income' without any immediate further liability to tax; and in the case of trusts, the capital sums withdrawn can be advanced by the trustees to the relevant beneficiaries with no personal tax charge.

In relating tax-wrappers to trusts, the key factor is that beneficiaries of 'interest in possession' (IIP) trusts have a right to income, but potential beneficiaries of discretionary trusts do not. Consequently, investment bonds are not suitable for IIP trusts, and trustees should instead consider using unit trusts, OEICs and investment trusts; or, if they prefer a 'passive', index-tracking, approach to investment, to low-charging exchange-traded funds.

The investment bond comes into its own when used as the vehicle for investments in discretionary trusts, in that it enables them to avoid the major tax hurdle which faces trustees who wish to distribute dividend income from such trusts.

Savings income is not an issue. Trustees are charged to income tax on savings income at the rate applicable to trusts (RAT) of 40 per cent, and because 20 per cent tax has been deducted at source, the trustees are liable for an additional 20 per cent tax. When this income is distributed to beneficiaries, the beneficiaries can recover from HMRC the difference between the tax paid by the trustees (40 per cent) and their own rate of tax.

By contrast, dividend income, when received by trustees, carries a 10 per cent tax credit and RAT is charged at 32.5 per cent instead of the normal rate of 40 per cent, and after taking account of the tax deducted at source, additional tax of 22.5 per cent is due. However, when this income is distributed to beneficiaries, it ceases to be regarded as dividend income for the purposes of tax credits and is regarded instead as income from a trust. In consequence, beneficiaries cease to able to claim the benefit of the dividend tax credit; and furthermore the income is still deemed for the purposes of the beneficiary's tax liability to have been franked at 40 per cent, even though the actual rate of tax was 32.5 per cent. The result is that all categories of taxpayer receiving dividend income from discretionary (and accumulation and maintenance) trusts suffer a 20 per cent higher tax charge than they would pay on savings income from the same trust. The higher rate taxpayer is in practice subject to a 46 per cent tax 'hit' in these circumstances.

Prima facie, income tax will be chargeable, potentially at the higher rate, on gains realised on the disposal of an investment bond by trustees. However, even this could be avoided if the trustees were to assign segments of the bond *in specie* to a non-higher rate taxpaying beneficiary or beneficiaries for nil consideration. The assignment would not constitute a chargeable event; and the beneficiary could proceed to encash the segments without any liability to tax.

The fact that investment bonds are non-income producing assets also offers administrative advantages and therefore further cost savings. If the whole of a trust fund is invested in a bond, no trust accounts are required, and for the years in which there is no chargeable event, the trustees' self-assessment form can be completed with a nil declaration for income tax and CGT.

The Trustee Act 2000, s.4(2) requires trustees to keep investments under review and s.5 requires them to take advice, except where this is unnecessary or inappropriate. Developments in products and markets and philosophies suggest there is plenty of scope for action on both these counts.

It should be noted that new tax rates will apply in 2011/12. The dividend trust rate will increase from 32.5 to 37.5 per cent and the RAT from 40 to 45 per cent, which will make the tax savings available through the use of an appropriate investment vehicle even more valuable.

14

Personal injury trusts and periodical payments

David Coldrick and Lynne Bradey

Introduction

Personal injury trusts are variously feared, misunderstood or just plain ignored by the legal advisers of personal injury victims. These are unhelpful reactions and, apart from letting clients down, they can render the personal injury lawyer liable for professional negligence claims either as the result of loss of benefits if there is no trust or because of problems arising in respect of inappropriately drafted trusts.

Benefits issues and other reasons for founding a personal injury trust

A person who has suffered a personal injury, whether by way of accident, disease or other cause, will often be receiving financial or practical assistance from the state. If a client is receiving means-tested benefits or local authority funded care, it is vital that they are advised that their benefits are likely to be affected (stopped or reduced) if they receive compensation but do not place their award into a personal injury trust.

There is a 'period of grace' of 52 weeks from the date of the first payment in respect of means-tested benefits but this does not apply to any later payments. Only the first payment will be disregarded from the means-testing calculation. This is in itself an often misunderstood complication. In larger cases, there will often be an interim payment. So for all but the smallest award, which will be spent quickly, it is unwise to rely upon it.

The main means-tested benefits which may be restricted or lost in the event that no trust is put in place are:

- Income Support;
- Income-based Jobseeker's Allowance (not to be confused with the National Insurance-based variant);
- Pension Credit Guarantee Credit;

- Council Tax Benefit;
- Housing Benefit.

From some of these benefits other advantages, such as free prescriptions, eye tests and dental care can follow.

New claims after October 2008, involving claimants who are unable to work, receive a means-tested version of a benefit called Employment and Support Allowance where they would previously have received Income Support. There is a National Insurance-based benefit of the same name, so care is needed.

The capital limits for most means-tested *income related* benefits (with the exception of Pension Credit) are £6,000 lower and £16,000 upper (2008–09). The capital limits for care related benefits are £13,500 lower and £22,250 upper.

Below the relevant lower capital limit the injured claimant will have a full entitlement and above the upper capital limit they will have no entitlement. But in cases involving income related benefits the capital of other members of the 'claimant unit', e.g. a cohabiting spouse, will be taken into account as part of the capital calculation.

Between the two upper and lower thresholds entitlement is reduced by a tariff income of £1 per week for every £250 above the lower capital limit.

However, advice on personal injury trusts does not only need to be given if a person is *currently* in receipt of means-tested benefits. A person may not be in current need of means-tested benefits but may potentially have access to them in the future if their assessable capital for means-testing purposes is low.

It should be remembered that provision for Long Term Care (at home or in a care home) is a means-tested benefit provided by local authorities. An injured client is more likely than others to need to take advantage of it in the future, e.g. in old age or if their health deteriorates on account of their injury.

The 'capital disregard' for Income Support and other means-tested benefits is contained in the Income Support (General) Regulations 1987, SI 1987/1967, Sched.10, para.12, (as amended). This states that:

> where the funds of a trust are derived from a payment made in consequence of any personal injury to the claimant, the value of the trust fund and the value of the right to receive any payment under that trust are disregarded.

There are also mirror provisions in paras 44(a) and 45(a) relating to personal injury compensation administered by the Court of Protection on behalf of a mentally incapable injured person.

Regulation 51(1)(a) of the Regulations also exempts a personal injury trust situation from the rules relating to 'deprivation of capital' and notional capital. These would usually impute a trust founded by a benefits claimant to that claimant: otherwise everyone would found a trust to enhance their entitlements. This recognises the special status of personal injury trusts.

Turning to Long Term Care, under the National Assistance (Assessment of Resources) Regulations 1992, SI 1992/2977, Sched.4, para.10, the following capital is to be disregarded:

> Any amount which would be disregarded under paragraph 12 of Schedule 10 to the Income Support Regulations (personal injury trusts).

This mirrors the regulations governing Income Support and other means-tested benefits. In addition, the deprivation of capital aspect of the notional capital rules does not apply when a person founds a personal injury trust. Usually if a person requiring care had founded a trust with the aim of reducing their liability to pay for their care, they could be treated as still owning the money in the trust fund. It would be assessed as notional capital and would be included when assessing how much capital the resident had.

Regulation 25(1)(a) of the 1992 Regulations states:

> A resident may be treated as possessing actual capital of which he has deprived himself for the purpose of decreasing the amount he may be liable to pay for his accommodation except:
>
> (a) where that capital is derived from a payment made in consequence of any personal injury and is placed on trust for the benefit of the resident . . .

It is clear that there can be significant advantages if a personal injury trust is founded.

There are also other positive advantages of personal injury trusts apart from the retention of means-tested benefits. These are often forgotten. That is particularly, but not exclusively, in the case of older, very young, mentally incapable or other vulnerable clients:

- They may have no experience of handling a large sum of money.
- They may want the protection which trustees can offer against grasping relatives.
- They may have unstable mental conditions which render the use of trustees helpful.
- They may just want to get on with their lives without having to concern themselves with financial administration.
- They may fear the impact of divorce and separation on their finances and want to try to 'ringfence' their resources in some way.

Choice of type of personal injury trust

The type of trust, and the name, are not important. Bare trusts, life interest trusts (flexible or otherwise) or discretionary trusts can be used as personal injury trusts. The two important points for benefits and care purposes are simply:

1. That there is a trust.
2. That it contains money which was paid as a result of a personal injury to the person claiming benefits.

Following the introduction of the Finance Act 2006, trusts have been categorised for tax purposes into two main groups: those which are part of the 'relevant property' regime and those which are not. The majority of personal injury trusts established are bare trusts which are transparent non-entities for tax purposes. A transfer into a bare trust attracts no inheritance tax charge, and income and capital gains are assessed on the founder or settlor of the trust, i.e. the injured party, in the present scenario.

By contrast, a transfer into a more complex discretionary trust (usually with several possible beneficiaries) or a life interest trust (usually for the injured settlor for life and then to others) will fall into the relevant property regime. In such cases a 20 per cent inheritance tax charge will be levied on the amount over the nil rate band for inheritance tax on entry into the trust. This is usually only triggered by mistake and is a source of numerous professional negligence claims.

For most people, a personal injury bare trust will be the simplest and most effective type of personal injury trust. For those who require greater protection, either from themselves or from others, a different type of trust may be more suitable. However, great care needs to be exercised, particularly when sums in excess of the nil rate band are involved. The alternatives are complex and beyond the scope of this brief overview.

The Court of Protection and personal injury trusts

It is possible to ask the Court of Protection to authorise the foundation of a personal injury trust on behalf of a person whose affairs would otherwise be dealt with by the court by dint of their mental incapacity. The motivation behind this is usually to provide a useful psychological separation from the court system for the injured person and their family.

At the time of writing, there are also significant service related issues in respect of the Office of the Public Guardian. Placing awards under control of 'private' personal injury trusts can therefore be highly desirable unless there are unusual vulnerabilities likely to require periodic recourse to the court – for example, where third party pressure is applied.

As the court is transferring responsibility it will wish to be assured that a suitable professional trustee is appointed, with experience in the administration of trusts for people who have been injured. Usually family members will also be trustees although occasionally a 'board of trustees' is considered, comprised exclusively of professionals.

The application for a personal injury trust is usually made by the court-appointed deputy for the injured person and will request that the court exercises its power under the Mental Capacity Act 2005, ss.16 and 18. As well as the court forms, assessment of capacity and a detailed statement in support of the application, it is advisable to include a supporting report by a suitably qualified professional.

It is also essential that a financial report is submitted. This report should usually be prepared on a fee basis by an independent financial adviser and should detail what the investment proposals would be if the application to establish a trust were granted.

Applications are dealt with on the papers, with the Official Solicitor appointed to act on behalf of the incapacitated person. The Official Solicitor may request changes to the deed or other aspects and if agreement is reached between the parties can recommend to the court that an order is made, authorising the execution of the trust deed.

Court of Protection applications are not required where an injured but mentally capable minor is involved. In such cases a trust can be founded under CPR rule 21.11. The same basic rationale and procedures apply, without the involvement of the Court of Protection.

Particular issues when investing for personal injury trusts

Perhaps the most important issue is that the trustees of a personal injury trust have the same responsibilities as the trustees of any other type of trust. That is despite the fact that they can usually be hired and fired by the injured person under the terms of a bare trust. In practice it is useful to secure the explicit agreement of the injured person to the proposed investment strategy wherever possible.

The majority of larger personal injury settlements will in future contain an element of regular periodical payments as well as a traditional lump sum award. This is particularly likely since the Courts Act 2003 came into effect in April 2005. This allowed the court to impose such payments without the consent of the parties. Previously, where consent was required, defendants would have to go to the market for an annuity or similar type of product to fund periodical payments unless they fell within the small category of organisations allowed to self-fund (such as the NHS Litigation Authority). This invariably worked out to be more expensive than the lump sum alternative.

Periodical payments are disregarded under the benefits and care regulations, but it can be useful to have these paid into a personal injury trust. Under benefits rules, income-type payments such as these are usually treated as capital at the end of the relevant period, e.g. after a year, in the case of an annual payment.

Periodical payments are not suitable for some types of damages, the most obvious of which is the one-off cost of purchasing and/or adapting a house. They can also be a poor fit with other recurring capital expenses. So lump sums will continue, as will the need for personal injury trusts.

15

Investing for clients who lack mental capacity

Adrian Mundell

The Mental Capacity Act 2005

The Mental Capacity Act 2005, which came fully into force on 1 October 2007, introduced a number of changes to the ways in which the affairs of those who have lost mental capacity are managed.

A key change was the replacement of enduring powers of attorney (EPAs) by lasting powers of attorney (LPAs), though EPAs made before 30 September 2007 remain valid. The terminology has also changed. The Public Guardianship Office, the administrative arm of the Court of Protection, has become the Office of the Public Guardian (OPG); and representatives appointed by the court to manage the affairs of persons who have lost the mental capacity to make decisions but have not made or registered a power of attorney are now known as deputies, rather than receivers.

LPAs can be for 'property and affairs' (i.e. financial), or 'welfare decisions' which need to be made on clients' behalf. Similarly, the powers given to a deputy may either be wide-ranging or be limited to an individual decision. So, the court can appoint a property and affairs deputy and/or a welfare deputy for a person without capacity where there is no power of attorney in place.

In addition to appointing deputies, the Court of Protection has the power:

- to decide whether a person has mental capacity to make a particular decision for themselves;
- to make decisions affecting people who lack mental capacity;
- to decide whether powers of attorney are valid;
- to remove deputies and attorneys who fail in their duties.

Once a deputy has been appointed, it is the responsibility of the OPG to monitor and supervise the deputy. The OPG website **www.public-guardian.gov.uk** explains the organisation's role, which includes:

- supervising deputies and attorneys (i.e. those appointed under power of attorney);
- providing reports to the court;
- setting up and managing a register of powers of attorney;
- setting up and managing a register of court orders appointing deputies (the OPG's registers may be searched subject to payment of a fee of £25).

The Act sets out a number of principles to assist in determining whether an individual may have lost mental capacity:

- Every adult has the right to make their own decisions and must be assumed to have capacity unless it is proven otherwise.
- People must be given all appropriate help before they can be considered unable to make their own decisions.
- Individuals have the right to make unwise decisions including decisions that others may consider eccentric.
- Anything done on behalf of a person who lacks capacity must be done in their best interests.
- Anything done on behalf of a person who lacks capacity should be the least restrictive on their basic rights and freedoms.

A Code of Practice accompanies the Act and provides additional guidance.

Consideration should be given to whether a person whose mental capacity is in doubt may be better able to make decisions at certain times of the day or in certain locations; whether information can be communicated to him or her in a more intelligible way, for example, by pictures, photos or sign language; whether all options have been fully communicated; and whether a third party such as a family member or friend may be able to assist the person in making a specific decision. It should also be borne in mind that the issue of capacity is decision-specific. A person may have the capacity to take a £10 note to a shop to buy some basic groceries, but may not be able to decide how a larger sum should be invested.

If there is reason to question whether a client possesses mental capacity, an opinion should be sought from their GP. This can be done by way of a COP3 'Assessment of Mental Capacity' form from the Court of Protection which may be downloaded from the OPG website.

Powers of attorney

If it has been established that a person lacks capacity and there is an EPA in place which has been registered at the Office of the Public Guardian, instructions can be taken from the attorney(s) who have been appointed.

Any action taken by the attorneys should be in the best interests of the protected person and if there is any reason to doubt the attorneys' actions these should be queried with the attorneys and possibly with the Court of Protection.

If an LPA is in place, the first step should be to check that this has been registered with the OPG. An LPA can only be used once it has been registered, unlike the old EPA. An LPA can be registered without the donor having lost capacity; but whether or not capacity has been lost, the donor should be involved in any decision-making process where possible.

Provided that there are no restrictions within the LPA, and that the requirements of the Mental Capacity Act 2005 have been met, instructions can be accepted from the attorney in respect of any investment decisions that need to be made.

Dealing with a deputy can be a different matter. Whereas an LPA is given by someone when they have capacity to make a decision as to who they want to act for them and any restrictions they want to place on that person, a deputy is appointed by the court for a person who has lost capacity without having appointed an attorney to act. The deputy acts on behalf of the protected person under the terms of an order of the court.

Types of court order

Under the transitional arrangements, all previous receiverships should automatically have been transferred to new deputyships but, as at the time of writing (September 2008), only a limited number have been transferred. There are also a variety of different types of order being issued by the court, with differing levels of authority being given to the deputies. Some orders are giving wide powers to the deputy in terms of dealing with investments, some requiring that 'The deputy must exercise such care and skill as is reasonable in the circumstances when investing the assets' (of protected persons) and others that 'The deputy may make any kind of investment that the person absolutely entitled to those assets could make', or that 'This general power of investment includes investment in land and investment in assets outside England and Wales'. Orders will then go on to talk about the need for the deputy to have regard to the standard investment criteria which apply to trusts, namely suitability and need for diversification and that the deputy must from time to time review the investments and consider whether they should be varied (although no timescale is set).

Orders issued by the court may state that the deputy must obtain and consider proper investment advice (meaning the advice of a person whom the deputy reasonably believes to be qualified to give it by their ability and practical experience). It is, however, a matter of some concern that the orders currently being issued are failing to require that the advice provided must be *independent* financial advice (though this requirement will apply to solicitor deputies by virtue of the Solicitors' Code of Conduct 2007). There is consequently a risk that lay deputies may fall prey to commission-hungry financial product salesmen.

Deputies and attorneys appointed on or after 1 October 2007, and receivers appointed before that date whose powers have been extended by the court to give them the same powers as deputies, are now permitted to manage clients' day-to-day financial matters without referring to the OPG. Prior to 1 October 2007, the Public Guardianship Office operated a panel of stockbrokers to which responsibility for the investment of clients' funds could be delegated, and special approval was required for the appointment of any other adviser (including independent financial advisers (IFAs)). However, the wider powers now given to deputies enable them to appoint financial advisers, from within their own firm or externally, without reference to the OPG. Consequently, the OPG no longer has direct dealings with investment advisers and investment proposals can be approved by deputies in cases where the terms of the court order allow this. In cases where the order does not allow this, it is the deputy who must apply to the court for approval.

In addition, investment advisers are no longer required to report to the OPG on the performance of investments, though the OPG may ask to see valuations and performance reports as part of deputies' annual reports.

Investment advisers' recommendations to deputies should take the form of a normal investment report and should suitably emphasise the importance of asset allocation in constructing portfolios. The proposed use of investment bonds is no longer frowned on, but the absence of commission bias must be made clear and advisers' remuneration should preferably take the form of fees. Until a recommendation is agreed, monies sit in the OPG's cash account but will be released at the request of a deputy.

Where the orders from the court are more restrictive there is an application process which must be followed. The forms involved are as follows.

Form COP1 'Application Form' will need to be completed, stating what order is being sought from the court. It is better to make the order as wide as possible to give flexibility. So, instead of asking the court to make an order that '£10,000 be invested into an ABC Ltd portfolio service', ask for an order that 'the deputy is authorised to make investment decisions based on advice from (IFA firm name)'.

Form COP24 'Witness Statement' will also need to be submitted, with the investment report attached, together with a cheque for the court's application fee which at the time of writing is £400. The statement should declare that the deputy has sought independent financial advice and should refer to the report, saying that the deputy feels that it is in the best interests of the protected person that the investments should be made. It should also refer to any involvement that the protected person may have had in making any decisions.

The current timescale from making an application to receiving an order is 21 weeks, but this may hopefully reduce as the court catches up on its back-log arising from the changes in the law. Specific investment recommendations may be subject to change during this period, so it would be prudent to build some flexibility into portfolio recommendations.

Family

16

Marriage, partnerships, separation and divorce

James Freeman and Clare Douglas

The impact of divorce on estate planning

At the time of writing, the current law in England and Wales as regards the division of the assets is far from clear-cut. Several aspects of the law are yet to be fully clarified. Consequently, negotiations and arguments can become very complicated, inevitably increasing costs, and this can particularly become the case in the hands of inexperienced lawyers.

That said, there is certainty in some areas. Bad behaviour or conduct is almost never going to be relevant to the financial outcome of a divorce. Whilst no doubt frustrating for the parties involved, the court is only interested in behaviour by the husband or the wife that is so serious that it really cannot be ignored, e.g. where one party has tried to kill or seriously injure the other or where the misconduct is specifically financial in nature.

The other (almost) certainty is that the 'bottom line' in terms of the division of assets on divorce is meeting the needs of the parties. 'Needs' means, in this situation, providing suitable accommodation and providing enough on which to live. Calculating needs is, in itself, a relatively straightforward exercise. However, it becomes more complicated where there are more significant assets such that there is likely to be an excess after 'needs' are met. The question then becomes how one divides this 'surplus wealth'.

Where there is surplus wealth, the presumption is an equal division of the capital on divorce and the key question then becomes '50/50 or why not?' According to case law, where there are surplus assets, there is a 'yardstick of equality' that should be applied. The court should therefore bear this in mind when determining the outcome, based upon the assets in question and the parties' respective needs.

The 50/50 presumption does not, however, apply in all cases. The length of the marriage is one determining factor. In short marriages where much of the wealth is accumulated by one of the parties prior to the marriage the likelihood is that there will be an unequal division of the assets. The court would, in all probability, look at what has been accumulated during the marriage itself (the 'marital acquest') and, subject to needs, divide that equally. In a 'long marriage' that is unlikely to apply and, in a medium length marriage it is very much a grey area (i.e. one of those aforementioned areas where there is a lack of clarity).

A second way in which the 50/50 presumption may not apply is where the paying party has successfully argued that they have made a 'special contribution' to the marriage. This is taken to mean that they have displayed such an extreme and unusual talent for generating wealth that it would not be fair for the results of that genius to be divided equally. Only a handful of people thus far have successfully argued that they fall within this category.

Apart from situations such as those described above, under English law as it currently stands, and despite a lack of clarity in several places, there is in effect a '50 per cent tax' rate applied to people with significant assets who are unfortunate enough to find themselves embroiled in a divorce.

Once the division of the capital assets has been determined, the question will need to be considered of whether ongoing financial support – i.e. maintenance – is required. It may be (depending on the circumstances) that, in addition to parting with a substantial proportion of their capital assets, the paying party may also have to provide ongoing financial support to their spouse. This could take the form of a regular monthly amount or an amount could be capitalised into a further lump sum.

Inevitably, because there are several unclear areas and all judges are different, matrimonial litigation can become both unpredictable and very costly. Accordingly, matrimonial practitioners will (or should) commonly attempt to negotiate a settlement without resorting to litigation.

No type of asset is automatically exempt from financial claims on divorce

Many different asset types can arise in matrimonial proceedings and almost all of them will be at risk on divorce, especially in a long marriage. These will include:

(a) **inheritances**, particularly if received during the marriage but also if received before the marriage, or even after the parties separate;

(b) **assets held in trust**, if a party has received a benefit from that trust. If, in reality, some or all of the trust assets are a resource of that party then most probably they will comprise part of the matrimonial 'pot', whether the trust is based onshore or offshore;

(c) **offshore assets**, including companies in foreign jurisdictions, holiday homes and the like;

(d) **business assets**, whether they are shareholdings in public companies or small, unlisted family businesses. With private companies and businesses there can be real issues about the value of that company/business, its liquidity and its true worth as an asset in the hands of one of the parties;

(e) **pensions** – these are often central to the settlement discussions and can commonly be subject to division by pension sharing order; and

(f) **pre-marital and post-separation assets**. The court is able to take into account assets that are accumulated before the marriage, especially in a long marriage, and can also include (at least to an extent) assets that have built up after separation but before the divorce is finalised. In this latter situation there can be very significant post-separation accruals, particularly where a couple has separated many years previously but never actually divorced at the time and one of the parties has benefited financially since the separation.

Divorcing clients may well need financial or wealth-management advice

The financial adviser (including the wealth manager) can play several very important roles if and when one of their clients is going through a divorce (or, in the civil partnership context, a dissolution). These are set out below.

(a) Funding for costs

The difficulty some clients face is not being able to afford legal representation, particularly when most, if not all, of the matrimonial assets are held in their spouse's or civil partner's sole name. In order to resolve this, some banks may be prepared to arrange a loan for clients for the purposes of professional divorce fees. A financial adviser is often well placed to assist with establishing this funding facility, providing financial information about the client and reviewing the terms and conditions of any loans that are offered.

(b) Information for disclosure

For the purposes of divorce, most clients find themselves having to complete, and exchange with the other party, a lengthy financial statement required by the court (known as a Form E). The ongoing nature of the relationship between financial adviser and client means that often they are best placed to gather together all the various pieces of financial information needed to complete this statement.

(c)   Tax advice

Tax advice also plays a critical role at various points in proceedings. Capital gains tax (CGT) issues may arise on the transfer of assets between the parties or on their sale, and advice should be taken on which assets should be transferred and when. Equally there may be inheritance tax (IHT) issues, particularly in respect of IHT planning after the divorce is finalised (when, of course, there will no longer be an exempt spouse available for planning purposes).

(d)   Financial review

The family lawyer might also need financial assistance when it comes to undertaking a review of the proposed settlement. It is all very well for the lawyers to formulate what they think would work as a legal settlement but the financial professional is likely to be better placed to assess whether, in reality, such a settlement will provide for all the financial needs of each party and also whether the income deriving from the lump sum is sufficient to meet the needs of the financially weaker party going forward.

(e)   Pensions advice

Pensions are often one of the most valuable assets in a divorce and, equally often, one of the least well understood by the lawyers. Expert advice from a financial adviser is often therefore very helpful. This advice could involve considering how best to split a pension; how the party receiving a pension share should best invest their pension; and how the party losing some of their pension can best rebuild the pot.

(f)   Investment advice post-settlement

Once the divorce settlement is finalised and implemented, it is common for the financially weaker party to walk away with, perhaps, a share of the other's pension and a lump sum. These assets need to be invested in such a way as to provide the required capital and income for that party, maybe for the rest of their life. This is not an area in which lawyers can advise.

Pre-nuptial agreements

Pre-nuptial agreements (PNAs) are not currently binding in the English courts. However, family judges are increasingly lending more weight to them, they are well constructed. There have been a number of recent cases where PNAs have been considered by the court as one of the factors to be taken into account when determining the division of the parties' assets. In the case of *Crossley* v. *Crossley* [2007] EWCA Civ 1467, the Court of Appeal essentially cut entirely the normal financial relief procedure owing to the existence of a PNA which provided that neither party would make a financial claim against the other if the marriage were to fall apart. Lord Justice Thorpe stated the following:

> If ever there is to be a paradigm case in which the court will look to the prenuptial agreement as . . . a factor of magnetic importance, it seems to me that this is just such a case.

A common intention behind a PNA in England is to attempt to ringfence two particular types of asset. The first is assets already owned by each of the parties at the date of the marriage or civil partnership. The second may broadly be described as 'family wealth', i.e. assets acquired by either party during the marriage by way of gift, inheritance or from trust (either a distribution from a trust or the receipt of an interest in a trust). It may well be advisable for the agreements to contain a confidentiality clause: high profile divorce cases tend to illustrate the value of discretion.

Certain factors need to be borne in mind to render a PNA as effective as possible. These were set out in the case of *K* v. *K (Ancillary relief: Prenuptial Agreement)* [2003] 1 FLR 120. Perhaps the most important of them are the following.

(a) Separate, good quality legal advice

Each party should have separate, good quality, specialist legal advice – and the lawyers on either side should be prepared to sign a certificate confirming that they have given such advice. Good practice suggests that the legal advice should be of a similar, high quality for each side and thus it is preferable to use firms that have a specialism in this area. Where clients approach a firm for advice about PNAs, whilst a general discussion about the legal basis for a PNA might perhaps be held with the couple together, from then on that firm can only advise one of the parties.

(b) Full financial disclosure

Each party to the PNA should provide full financial disclosure so as to avoid any argument that the financially weaker party would not have entered into the agreement had he or she known the full extent of the other party's wealth. If the parties were in the process of divorcing, full details of all assets, together with supporting documentation, would have to be disclosed to the other. The counsel of perfection would be to provide a similar level of disclosure when negotiating a PNA. However, the practicalities of this sort of exercise, from both a time and cost perspective, often mean that a summary of the asset position, sometimes referring to bands of wealth, is provided instead. With reference to earlier comments on the role of the financial adviser, this is certainly another area in which one can become involved in the process.

(c)   Reasonable terms

The terms of the PNA need to be fair and reasonable. The needs of each party should always be provided for as a minimum, and particularly the needs of any child or children.

(d)   No pressure

There should be no pressure on either party to sign the PNA. Such pressure might come from the other party or perhaps their family. It might also include pressure of time. Good practice accordingly suggests that there should be a 'cooling off' period of at least 21 days between the date of the agreement and that of the marriage (or civil partnership). This period is by no means set in stone, but is a useful guide.

Considering the impact of divorce on the next generation

It can be disappointing for the older generations if, when the family wealth is devolved in a tax-efficient way, a member of the next generation goes through a difficult divorce and a large slice of the family wealth is passed to his or her (ex)spouse. One way in which such a scenario could be avoided might be to ask that each member of the next generation (if they wish to participate in family wealth) enters into a PNA before getting married. Where wealth is held in trust structures, consideration should be given to the terms and operation of the trust and the content of any letters of wishes.

Lifetime gifts carry an obvious danger when the recipient's marriage might founder after receipt of the gift.

The possible impact of matrimonial planning on trust structures

Treatment of trusts by the courts

Judicious encouragement orders

An 'encouragement order' obliges the paying party to make financial provision for the other party in a quantum which is premised on assistance being given to the paying party from the trust. This may be particularly relevant where the paying party resides in England and Wales but the trust is situated offshore. It also tends to be the preferred approach of the courts of the Family Division.

Variation orders

The courts have jurisdiction to vary nuptial trusts under the Matrimonial Causes Act 1973, s.24 and that jurisdiction extends to trusts governed by foreign jurisdictions: the power to vary arises from the English courts' jurisdiction in divorce proceedings rather than the governing law of the trust. It will therefore make no difference if the trust has an exclusive jurisdiction clause specifying a jurisdiction other than England.

'Nuptial trust' is not a strictly defined term, but it is likely that any trust settled in contemplation of or during the marriage could fall into this category.

Enforcement of variation orders abroad is a different matter. Historically, some foreign jurisdictions have been more accommodating than others in accepting variation orders from the English court. This has been brought into focus in the case of *Charman* v. *Charman* [2006] 1 WLR 1053. In this case a trust of considerable value was moved to Bermuda before divorce proceedings began in England. Some offshore jurisdictions tend to be robust in declining to enforce foreign orders; others less so.

In general, the courts of the Family Division will attempt to make fair provision for a spouse without interfering with the terms of a trust. If the trust has to be varied, the court will vary it to the least extent necessary to produce a fair resolution and will consider other beneficiaries in doing so. There must also be a realistic prospect of enforcing the order to vary.

Discretionary trusts

In the case of self-settled discretionary trusts, the court will treat the trust fund as though it were capital in the hands of the settlor beneficiary (presuming that the settlor is a beneficiary). If the trust is not self-settled then the court will look to the letter of wishes, if there is one, and may well treat the husband or wife beneficiary as having the benefit contemplated by the settlor in that letter. This will therefore be a crucial document. If there is no such letter of wishes then the court will look at how the trust has operated in the past to find a pattern from which it can ascribe a value to the benefits that the party is likely to receive from the trust. Courts are used to powers of advancement within discretionary trusts being used to provide a party with capital to which that party would not otherwise have access. Courts will look closely at the provisions and historical operation of any such powers in order to decide whether the trust is a 'resource' of one of the beneficiaries.

Does the settlor need to be a beneficiary?

Where a party clearly has surplus wealth, it might be an idea to raise with him or her the question of whether they really need to be a beneficiary. A settlor does not necessarily need to benefit under the trust and indeed can choose to be excluded as a beneficiary under it. In the case of *Charman*, both parties were excluded beneficiaries under the trust that was not in contention, namely the children's trust, and no one sought to argue that the value of this trust should be added to either party's side of the balance sheet. Trustees need very careful advice before thinking of exercising powers to exclude a beneficiary if divorce proceedings are mooted or commenced.

Jurisdiction should always be considered

Choice of jurisdiction

Choice of jurisdiction is important, several jurisdictions now having trust legislation in place expressly stating that orders of foreign courts in respect of divorce proceedings and asset division are not to be enforced. This highlights the fact that obtaining an English divorce order may be one thing but enforcing the order can be quite another matter. However, it is important to consider that, although certain jurisdictions may have such protective legislation in place, such jurisdictions need also to have a sufficiently well-developed trust industry to enable the trust to be properly managed. There is no point in selecting a protective jurisdiction for divorce related reasons if the majority of trust assets are situated within the English jurisdiction and/or the trust is poorly run in the meantime.

Enforceability

Where the trust's assets, or some of them, are located within the English jurisdiction, it is usually relatively straightforward to enforce an order of the English court against them. Where the assets are not in England and Wales, however, the location of the trust becomes all important.

As with other offshore assets, the court may refuse to vary an offshore trust if, on the evidence, it is not likely to be possible to enforce it (*Hamlin* v. *Hamlin* [1986] 1 FLR 61). Some offshore jurisdictions take a robust stand against variation orders from the English courts. However, even if a jurisdiction has a policy of non-enforcement of foreign matrimonial orders, this does not prevent steps being taken against trustees in the local court, for example in relation to disclosure for declaration of a sham trust under local law.

Other wealth protection techniques

Post-nuptial agreements

Post-nuptial agreements take much the same form as PNAs save that, as is perhaps self-evident, they are entered into once the marriage has taken place. Commonly either the parties did not have sufficient time before the wedding to draw up a PNA (and were perhaps also conscious that they did not want there to be an argument of pressure of time) or else they married some time ago, since when the law relating to finances on divorce has changed significantly from what they expected. Another possibility is that the marriage may have encountered difficulties and the spouses wished pre-emptively to deal with the financial consequences of breakdown – though caution is required in such circumstances.

The status of the post-nuptial agreement has recently been clarified and enhanced by the decision of the Privy Council in the case of MacLeod [2008] UKPC 64. As a species of maintenance agreement under the Matrimonial Causes Act 1973, such agreements will essentially be binding on the spouses save where they do not provide properly for a child or where there has been a change in the circumstances which prevailed at the time the agreement was concluded. This potential to be actually binding differentiates the post-nuptial agreement from the PNA. It will be advisable for couples to consider carefully whether they wish to re-endorse their PNA after the marriage in order to achieve the greatest possible level of certainty.

Cohabitation agreements

Properly drawn, a cohabitation agreement is a legally binding contract between two parties who decide to live together but not to marry or register a civil partnership. In such an agreement, they exchange promises as to how financial elements of their relationship will be arranged and conducted. The agreement gives cohabitants the opportunity to determine the consequences of separation for themselves. It also may allow those in more vulnerable positions to secure for themselves rights that they would otherwise not have, most obviously rights to a share of the equity in the family home and ongoing financial support from their former partner. Such agreements may also contain a useful confidentiality clause. It is likely to be good practice to provide financial disclosure prior to the signing of such as agreement.

For those cohabitants who do subsequently marry, a cohabitation agreement is a useful precursor to a PNA and will assist in establishing a 'course of dealings' between the parties.

Family protocols

A family protocol is an ongoing agreement to which members of a family may be asked to subscribe on attaining majority, in order to participate in the family wealth. The protocol may oblige each family member to enter into a PNA before getting married, a cohabitation agreement if they intend to cohabit and perhaps to have in place certain will or trust arrangements. It may also assist in defining the roles that family members will play in relation to, for example, a family business, and may contain confidentiality provisions.

17

Collaborative divorce

John Porteous

Collaborative family law is a new approach pioneered to manage the divorce and separation process in a more consensual manner than the traditional court route.

In this collaborative process, the family lawyers and their clients agree to reach settlement without the need for court orders. The parties work together to resolve issues, in particular custody and financial, arising out of the separation. During this process, 'experts' may be enlisted, such as financial specialists who will become part of the collaborative team.

Specialist advice from private client lawyers will continue to be needed in the same way as in traditional divorces and separations. This 'collaborative team', utilising their collective skills in client representation, negotiation and problem-solving, can help their clients shape and reach a fair agreement.

Why choose the collaborative process?

Relationship breakdown will always involve financial and emotional costs. The benefits of the collaborative approach help minimise those costs for all concerned. The reasons some may choose to pursue the collaborative process for divorce are:

- The parties are in control of the outcome and involved at every stage. The collaborative team keeps the process on track as well as providing legal advice, guidance and financial planning clarity.
- It takes the specific interests of both parties into consideration instead of the court deciding which issues are most important.
- The time the process takes depends on the parties' timetable. This can be quicker than the court timetable, but could also allow time for counselling, sale of a company, children to finish exams or other issues that the couple agree are important.
- The financial neutral can play a key role in the financial settlement to help both parties understand their individual financial position now and the realistic options available.

- The collaborative team works towards creating a settlement and cannot go to court for the matter to be resolved. The collaborative process is therefore not approached in the adversarial way required by the court process.
- The process makes it much easier for the couple to maintain ongoing relationships, such as if they have children and mutual friends or if they wish to continue to run a business together, as it aims to maintain lines of communication.
- The process keeps the children out of the crossfire and hopefully keeps what antagonism there is to a minimum. The couple may also find it easier to resolve any issues regarding the children through the collaborative process.
- It can cost less than the traditional fully litigated process.

While this offers some couples a less painful process of separating, it is not suitable for everyone. The parties must be committed to the process and confident they will both be honest about their own financial situation. Some couples will find it too difficult to be so directly involved and, in particular, to attend meetings with their soon to be ex-partner.

These couples may prefer their lawyers and other advisers to deal with the separation for them.

The collaborative process at work

Couples who believe the collaborative process could work for them will both meet individually with their separate lawyers. The process then involves 'four-way meetings', at which the couple and their respective lawyers are present.

It has become increasingly common for these four-way meetings to extend to five-way meetings as the parties seek a financial neutral to be present, helping the parties understand the financial issues arising from the separation.

Each meeting is used to deal with specific issues, moving the process forward in a structured manner. In straightforward cases, between two and four meetings are likely to be enough. Once an agreement has been reached, it is drawn up in a legally binding document and must be approved by the court.

It is not necessary for the couple or their lawyers to attend court in most cases, with the court process being managed through the postal service.

To benefit from the collaborative process, the participants must feel they have an open forum to discuss their concerns freely. This will help everyone to develop an understanding of the couple's financial position, the realistic options available and understand the full implications of the financial settlement.

The gathering and interpretation of this information is crucial to the entire process. It allows the parties to agree to a workable and mutually beneficial solution.

It is important to remember that if no settlement is reached during the collaborative process, new lawyers and financial consultants will have to be instructed for any court proceedings to begin.

Commitment must be gained early on from both parties to ensure the process is successful.

The role of the financial consultant/neutral

For this process to work effectively, in many cases there is a need for a neutral party to facilitate such discussion and ideally this falls to a financial consultant who has no existing loyalty to either of the divorcing parties.

Where all parties agree, the financial consultant can operate as a financial neutral. They may participate in the five-way meetings or see the couple individually or together.

The financial neutral is a valuable partner to the process in many cases. The experience in North America over the past 17 years shows that the introduction of the financial consultant at the start of the collaborative process enables both parties to have financial clarity from the beginning, removing antagonism later on in the process.

The UK lags behind the US in this regard, with financial neutrals typically being brought in to deal with specific queries or to act on a court instruction.

The financial consultant will help both parties fully understand the divorcing parties' financial position by creating a financial planning strategy and through dialogue, interpretation and education allow the process to continue to an agreed financial settlement.

This can be an involved process, especially around final salary pension benefits and necessitates their inclusion at an early stage in the collaborative process.

While the role of a financial neutral can provide significant clarity and support for an individual who has chosen the collaborative approach, their service is equally of value for the traditional divorce route.

Consideration should be given by both parties to involve an accredited divorce specialist in their negotiations to help them understand and evaluate the value of a number of the matrimonial assets.

Removing conflicts of interest

To avoid any conflict of interest or accusations of bias, it is imperative that the financial consultant does not implement any of the agreed settlement options, nor should they benefit from the payment of commissions or gain funds under management.

The financial consultant should not have had a previous or have an existing relationship with the parties outside the collaborative process.

Selecting a financial consultant

When selecting a suitable financial consultant to act as the financial neutral, it is important to recognise that the consultant should possess the necessary technical and professional skills, particularly in the areas of pensions, pension transfers, investments and family protection. They should also be familiar with the legal process.

Resolution is the national body for specialist family lawyers (**www. resolution.org**) and has pioneered an accreditation process for financial consultants. The financial consultants with the requisite qualification can apply to Resolution to undertake the rigorous training and testing process to become a Resolution Accredited Divorce Specialist.

Given the need for the collaborative team to work together at the highest level, Resolution has developed an accreditation system for suitably qualified financial planners. This demonstrates that the individual has a thorough understanding of the issues involved in family law and is qualified to provide advice in the collaborative environment.

While it is not compulsory to use an accredited financial consultant, the early indications are that the family law community will look to this as a benchmark of competence.

18

Care fees planning

Janet Davies

Current legislation

If someone needs to move into a care home what government support can they expect? If they have capital over the upper threshold level they will not qualify for assistance from the local authority until such a time as their capital might fall below this amount. Financial thresholds vary from country to country within the UK:

Country	Upper threshold	Lower threshold
England	£22,250	£13,500
Wales	£22,000	£19,000
Scotland	£21,500	£13,000
Northern Ireland	£22,000	£13,250

Most savings and assets are included in the means test, but some confusion has surrounded the subject of whether or not a person's home is included. It will be excluded only if:

- the spouse still resides in the home; or
- a relative over 60 resides in the house; or
- a disabled relative lives at the property; or
- a child under 16 lives in the property; or
- the person is in the first 12 weeks of needing permanent care; or
- the care is being provided on a temporary basis.

Private care fees have to be met from existing capital and income.

The exclusion of the home from the means test for the first 12 weeks following admission to a care home (once a permanent contract is established) means that if the remaining capital falls inside the current threshold the local authority should assist with the payment of care fees. It is worth noting that authorities will in most cases only pay up to their published limits, which could leave a family with what is known as a 'third party top up', to cover any difference in actual care fees and the local authority contribution. The money paid out by the local authority during the first 12 weeks is not normally repayable.

If, after the first 12 weeks, the property has not been sold, the local authority can continue to pay towards the care fees, under the 'deferred payment agreement' or 'Government Loan Scheme', but this money is repayable once the property is sold.

State benefits

Most state benefits are means-tested. However, Attendance Allowance is a non-means tested, tax-free state benefit, payable to all individuals over the age of 65 who are in need of care (defined as help with essential daily tasks, such as washing and dressing) for longer than six consecutive months.

Attendance Allowance is available at two rates: a lower rate, for those who need help during the day or the night; and a higher rate, for those needing care during both the day and night.

Individuals under the age of 65 who need care will still qualify for an allowance, but this will be paid in the form of Disability Living Allowance.

Following the implementation of the Health and Social Care Act 2001, individuals assessed as needing nursing care in a nursing home are entitled to receive an additional nursing care allowance; this is officially known as RNCC (Registered Nursing Care Contribution). This allowance is non-means tested and tax free, although how much is paid will depend on where the claimant lives.

Country	Amount (per week)
England	£103.80
Wales	£117.63
Scotland	£ 67.00
Northern Ireland	£100.00

A person may in addition qualify for Continuing Care, whereby the NHS contributes to the cost of care. However, to qualify for this benefit, patients must be unstable and/or unpredictable and need constant 24-hour specialist/ acute nursing care. The primary care trust (PCT) will carry out a Continuing Care assessment on request.

It is important to note that no nursing care allowance is currently payable for people classified as needing residential care (in a care home without nursing) or for those people receiving care in their own home.

NHS Continuing Care and Personal Care

In recent years, several test case families have been in the headlines for successfully pursuing claims against the PCT for Continuing Care payments. These may have been the tip of the iceberg as anecdotal evidence suggests that up to three-quarters of elderly people meeting the criteria are missing out on NHS funding.

The need for clarity here was paramount, and the government did respond by clarifying the rules and eligibility for Continuing Care. More and more people are now being awarded Continuing Care; and retrospective claims can now be made for Continuing Care payments going back to 1 April 1996, including claims in respect of the deceased.

Personal Care is only available in Scotland and is currently paid at £149 per week. Should a resident qualify for Personal Care, they would no longer be eligible to receive Attendance Allowance.

CRAG

The *Charging for Residential Accommodation Guide* (CRAG), which provides guidance to local authorities on charging for residential accommodation, is to be completely rewritten and may well result in a change in capital thresholds. In addition, the October 2007 pre-budget report contained a pledge that the government would produce a Green Paper in 2008 on the future funding of long-term care. It is now expected that this will be published in 2009 and will address the following issues:

- a revision of means-testing rules, possibly making the thresholds significantly higher;
- the closure of the current loop-hole of using insurance bonds to shelter assets;
- the reintroduction of a dedicated Long Term Care insurance policy;
- the combination of equity release and Long Term Care.

Financial solutions

Since Long Term Care (LTC) became recognised as an issue in the 1980s, there have been three types of product which have been available to provide funding:

- LTC investment bonds;
- LTC insurance policies;
- immediate needs annuities.

LTC investment bonds and LTC insurance policies have not proved to be popular and have been withdrawn from the market, leaving immediate needs annuities as the principal insurance-based solution. Indeed, the market for these products has flourished as underwriting has become increasingly bespoke. As their name suggests, they are suitable for individuals with an immediate need for income to fund the cost of care.

Immediate needs annuities are essentially similar to conventional purchased life annuities, but they can be arranged so that the income is paid to a registered care provider (care home or home care agency), in which case the total benefit is completely tax free for the policyholder. Policies can alternatively be arranged so that the policyholder receives the money direct, and this option is often preferred by those who may have elected to remain in their own home with an informal care arrangement. However, part of each payment will in this case be subject to tax at source, though the taxable element is likely to be relatively small, because it is the capital element which is tax free and this will be greater in the case of an impaired life (the shorter the likely payment period, the greater will be the proportion of each payment which represents a return of capital).

However, as the following case study shows, this is a field in which holistic financial planning is required, and if insurance products are used they are likely to provide only part of the solution. No two client scenarios are the same, and the advice and recommendations will need to be tailored to clients' individual requirements.

CASE STUDY

Russell and Kim Carter were anxious to sort out the continued care fees for Russell's mum, who at 83 had been showing signs of some memory loss and a series of falls necessitated a stay in hospital, and although her health improved slightly, her family did not believe that she could continue to live safely in her own home.

The family found a care home with which they were all happy and Mrs Carter moved in for a trial period. Once the care became permanent the family wanted to make sure that Mrs Carter could stay in this home for the rest of her life; and they also wanted to make sure that she need not worry about her money. Mrs Carter herself also had concerns. She wanted to leave some of her money as an inheritance to her family, and she was worried that her care bills would prevent this.

Local authority help with care fees is rigorously means-tested and as Mrs Carter had over £22,250 in capital and income she would not qualify for any continued assistance (£22,250 corresponds to the 2008/09 local authority thresholds for England).

The family sold the property and implemented a structured financial plan. The important part of any care fees planning exercise is to establish several key points, making sure that the actual plan, the monthly benefit level and the premium method match each individual circumstance, and this was how Mrs Carter's requirements were calculated:

Capital	
House sale and savings	£140,000

Income	
Including her basic state pension (with Age Allowance), private pension, Attendance Allowance and standard RNCC	£ 13,831

Expenses	
Care fees of £527 per week and incidental expenses @ £20 per week	£ 28,444

This left Mrs Carter with a deficit between her income and expenses of £14,613.

The Carter family wanted guaranteed peace of mind and the reassurance that the money should never run out, and in order to achieve this they purchased an immediate care plan for Mrs Carter, which cost £48,567.

The plan now pays the care home £14,613 each year (plus annual increases of 5 per cent) for the rest of Mrs Carter's life, which pleased Mrs Carter as she now knows that her family will receive the inheritance that she wished to leave them, and the family know that Mrs Carter should never run out of money, no matter how long she might need care.

19

Equity release

Ian Muirhead

Equity release is becoming an increasingly popular way for retired people to supplement their pensions. There are two types of scheme: reversion schemes and lifetime mortgages.

Reversion schemes

These schemes allow homeowners to sell all or part of their property to a reversion company and be granted a rent-free lifetime tenancy. The provider either pays a lump sum when the transaction is completed, or pays a regular annuity income for the life of the homeowner. The value received depends on the age of the homeowner, but it will always be much less than the value of the property, reflecting the fact that no rent is payable by the homeowner, and the provider has to wait until the planholder's death before recovering the value of its investment. The longer the homeowner lives, the better the deal becomes from their point of view. People in poor health can secure more favourable terms and the market is developing for impaired life equity release products. When eventually the property is sold, the reversion company keeps the sale value of its share, while the value of the retained share goes to the estate of the homeowner.

The main advantage of these schemes is certainty. The homeowner has a clear idea of the final cost when entering into the plan. It is based on a percentage of the value of the property. The balance of the value of the property will be retained for the benefit of the homeowner's estate. Disadvantages of some home reversion schemes are that the homeowner would lose out if either he or she died prematurely or house prices rose significantly. However, some schemes now offer protection against both these eventualities, and provide guarantees that a minimum payment will be made on death or removal from the property within an initial period of four years; and that if the property value increases by more than 7.5 per cent a year above the rate of inflation during the term of the scheme, the excess will be shared equally between the planholder and the reversion provider.

If the plan is taken out by a single person, their home will be sold when they die and the planholder's proportion of the value of the property will pass to their estate. When the plan is taken out by a couple, it will be arranged on a joint life basis and the property will not be sold until after the second death.

All reversion schemes are portable, but there can be difficulties if the homeowner decides to move to a less valuable property, and in any event the new property will need to meet the reversion company's criteria.

Lifetime mortgages

These are interest-only mortgages, with a rate of interest which is fixed (or capped) for life, but there is no fixed repayment period. Interest rolls up until the capital is repaid: on death; on moving into long-term care; or on the sale of the property. Then, capital and interest are repaid and the balance of the value of the home goes to the estate. Any existing mortgage must be repaid as the new lender takes a first charge on the property.

Homeowners receive an amount of money on completion of the mortgage, which can be taken in the form of a lump sum or can be applied to purchase an annuity which will provide a regular income. If income is required, the financial adviser will review the rates offered by competing lenders. The amount of the loan will then be dictated by the amount of income required. Some lenders allow the loan to be drawn down in tranches, so that interest is only paid on what has been drawn. This also provides protection against the risk to the homeowner of spending capital on buying an annuity and then dying prematurely and losing the capital invested. This arrangement also avoids income tax, because each payment received is an advance of capital.

The maximum amount which can be borrowed is determined by the age of the homeowner, who must be at least 60. Over an extended loan period the combined value of capital and interest could exceed the value of the home, particularly if house prices stagnate. However, lenders now offer a 'no negative equity' guarantee, which ensures that the homeowner will never owe more to the lender than the value of their property. The cost of providing this guarantee is the reason why a higher rate of interest is often charged on lifetime mortgages compared with other types of mortgage, though greater competition has driven down the rate differential.

Once the lifetime mortgage scheme starts, the amount borrowed against the property can often only be changed if provision is made for this in the mortgage terms. Similarly, the rate at outset may remain unchanged for the life of the plan – unlike the general mortgage market, where rates are usually flexible. This means that assuming an average mortgage rate around 6 per cent per annum, the mortgage debt under a lifetime mortgage would double every 12 years.

Unlike reversion schemes, only the homeowner benefits from any increase in house prices under a lifetime mortgage arrangement. Homeowners rely on increases in value to pay the rolled-up interest on their loans. However, the amount which will be owed by the planholder's estate to the provider cannot be predicted, because it depends on a number of factors, including the length of time the planholder lives, the level of interest rates and the level of house price inflation. The Consumers' Association has calculated that planholders could end up owing more than six times the amount they borrow if they live a long time, depending on the rate applied. So, clients with a family history of longevity might be better suited by reversion schemes. Conversely, if the homeowner died only one month after taking out a lifetime mortgage, only one month's interest plus the amount of the loan would be payable. Reversion schemes provide greater certainty as to the costs and benefits.

There are different approaches to early repayment charges. Some providers impose fixed redemption penalties, and others have charges which are geared to prevailing interest rates. The latter introduce an element of uncertainty. They could be less expensive than fixed rates when interest rates are declining, but more expensive when they are increasing.

Solicitors' involvement

Solicitors may recall the Home Income Plan mis-selling scandal in the late 1980s, when many borrowers suffered loss as a result of negative equity and solicitors were caught up in the claims for compensation. Since then, safeguards have been introduced to protect consumers against a repetition of the problems, but these place greater responsibility on financial advisers and solicitors.

A solicitor who acted for defendants in the leading case arising out of the mis-selling, *Investors' Compensation Scheme* v. *West Bromwich Building Society* [1998] 1 WLR 896, commented in the Law Society's *Gazette* on 4 September 2003 'although many of the claims against solicitors in the 1990s failed, higher standards of care could be imposed on solicitors now as a result of subsequent case law'. He went on 'solicitors acting for elderly clients on equity release schemes should think carefully about their risk management, as sometimes their beneficiaries can develop 20/20 hindsight when they see the downside of the schemes in a few years' time'. This concern is reinforced by the Financial Services Authority, which has emphasised to financial advisers the potential vulnerability of equity release clients and the need for specialist qualifications. From this point of view, the Consumers' Association has suggested that equity release schemes should be regarded as 'an option of last resort'.

In the *West Bromwich* case, a possible cause of action against lenders, financial advisers and solicitors identified by the court was a claim for damages in respect of loss suffered on account of entering into the transaction, which might have included: money lost on an ill-advised investment; fees paid to advisers for extricating the householder from his predicament; high rates of interest paid to the building society; and money spent under the impression that this could be afforded. Another cause of action against lender and/or solicitors might have been participation in misrepresentations made by the financial adviser.

Safe Home Income Plans

Most of the providers of equity release plans are members of the self-regulatory organisation Safe Home Income Plans (SHIP) and agree:

(a) to disclose in their literature all costs, the position on moving home, tax liabilities and the effect on the scheme of changing house values, and to issue certificates showing how the loan amount will change over time and whether a part or all of the property is being sold. It will also state the total cost to the householder's assets and estate;

(b) that clients' legal work will always be performed by the solicitor of their choice. The solicitor will not be chosen by the product provider. The solicitor must sign a certificate confirming that the scheme's legalities were explained to the client and that the solicitor is independent of both the lender and the financial adviser and has neither received nor offered any financial remuneration to the financial adviser;

(c) that if planholders wish to move home SHIP members will permit transferability of equity release schemes by guaranteeing to provide an equivalent facility based on the new home;

(d) that lifetime mortgage schemes carry a 'no negative equity' guarantee, which ensures that the cost of the loan plus accrued interest at the death of the planholder will never exceed the value of the property.

There is no standard wording for the SHIP certificate, whose terms vary from one provider to another. However, it is important that solicitors should ensure that certificates are completed correctly, because no SHIP plan can proceed without the certificate. Research by SHIP has indicated that 25 per cent of SHIP certificates are returned by planholders' solicitors without being completed properly or signed – which inevitably causes delays.

Most equity release providers insist that all non-owning occupiers aged 17 or over must sign an occupier's deed and seek separate legal advice. When an equity release property is not occupied by the planholder, and the occupier is physically or mentally incapable, the equity release provider will usually require written confirmation from the financial adviser and the occupier's GP that arrangements have been made for the occupier to be cared for at other premises in the event of the planholder dying or permanently leaving the property.

Equity release providers will usually accept documents executed under an enduring or lasting power of attorney if the planholder is mentally incapacitated, subject to registration. Where the planholder is physically incapacitated and an enduring power of attorney is in place, this need not be registered but the solicitor must provide confirmation that both the planholder and the attorney have received advice.

Tax and state benefits

To the extent that the homeowner elects to draw income from an equity release scheme, the payments are made from a purchased life annuity. Consequently, the proportion of the 'income' which is provided by means of a return of capital is tax free, but the balance is subject to income tax. Furthermore, the income element of each payment will be added to the basic state pension for the purposes of calculating state benefits; and it will also count against Age Allowance.

Instead of taking either a lump sum or an income, some plans permit a monthly cash drawdown option, which is not subject to income tax. However, this can be less efficient for inheritance tax. The value of the planholder's estate will be reduced for inheritance tax purposes by the amount of the mortgage debt or the equity relinquished. However, the costs involved make it unlikely that these schemes will be used purely as an estate planning tool.

V

Corporate

20

Pensions and estate planning for business proprietors

Steve Patterson

Vehicles for individual pensions

Personal pensions came into existence in 1988. At one end of the range are 'employer sponsored' group personal pensions (GPPs), which provide employees with pension arrangements that, in theory at least, are 'portable' from one employment to the next. These were initially popular with businesses and offered a simpler alternative to occupational pension schemes, which are subject to more stringent legal requirements and obligations, to say nothing of the more complex tax treatment, including constraints on benefits which are subject to HMRC restrictions based on salary and service with the relevant employer.

Group personal pensions are simply a collection of individual personal pensions administered on a collective basis by the 'provider' (normally, but not necessarily, an insurance company) with monthly premiums collected centrally through the employer's payroll system. Each individual plan is effectively 'owned' by the employee and can be taken with him or her on to their next employment.

This is fine in theory, provided the next employer is willing to contribute to an individual pension plan that is not part of its own GPP or occupational scheme. In practice, few employers have been happy with the arrangement, anticipating the problems that would arise from the need for multiple payments to different pension companies with unwieldy if not downright impossible administrative control through computerised payroll systems.

Nevertheless, the government of the day was intent on giving individuals greater control over their retirement provision and many employers were happy to switch from the more complex occupational schemes to GPP arrangements, which have grown in popularity ever since.

Self-employed people, including partners in professional firms, had always needed to make their own individual arrangements, and until the introduction of personal pensions would have invested in retirement annuity contracts, which are often described as the predecessor of personal pensions. Although no new retirement annuity plans could be established after 1988, many people maintained their existing policies and many of these are still in existence. In our experience it is not unusual for professional clients and self-employed businessmen to have accumulated a mixture of personal pensions and retirement annuities by the time they reach retirement.

Some retirement annuities offer valuable benefit guarantees, for example guaranteed annuity rates that were written into the original policy conditions. At the time these policies were designed, interest rates and therefore annuity rates were far higher than they are nowadays and we have seen some policies offering terms almost twice as attractive as annuity providers currently offer on the open market.

Personal pensions have increased in flexibility over the years. The two most significant improvements were the introduction of 'self-invested' personal pensions (SIPPs) in 1990 and the introduction of 'pension drawdown' in 1995. These were seismic changes for individual retirement planning and both variants have grown enormously in popularity over the intervening years.

For a number of years before the introduction of personal pensions the concept of 'self-investment' within a pension plan had existed through a special type of company occupational scheme for private (director controlled) businesses, known as 'small self-administered schemes' (SSASs).

Like their larger occupational scheme counterparts, these were generally established under trust and also subject to a separate legal framework known as the 'scheme rules', in much the same way as a company operates under a set of rules in the form of its Memorandum and Articles of Association. Whereas a company is run by its directors, a pension scheme is run by trustees who have powers and duties as described in the trust deed and scheme rules, which must in turn conform with the relevant underlying legislation. SSASs became particularly popular with profitable private businesses – often family controlled companies or companies run by two or three directors.

Pension scheme investment in property

The main attraction of SSASs was that instead of the company paying pension contributions on behalf of its directors into an insurance company fund, which in turn would invest in a range of assets such as commercial property and quoted shares, the SSAS pension fund could invest back into the directors' own business and be used to purchase business premises.

Although such schemes could acquire shares in the employer the more typical route for self-investment has taken the form of a 'loan back' arrangement, under which up to 50 per cent of the asset value of the fund could be reinvested back into the business as a commercial loan.

Profitable companies were therefore able to shelter profits from tax through pension contributions while recycling a proportion of the sheltered profit back into the business in return for which the company would pay interest at a commercial rate to its pension fund. The balance of the fund would often be invested in insurance polices for the director, held in the name of the trustees.

The second major investment opportunity has been to use the fund to acquire business premises. Where required, the trustees are permitted to borrow funds within specified limits for this purpose. In many cases the directors' existing pension policies would be transferred into the SSAS to provide the initial capital in addition to fresh contributions from pre-tax profits.

This enabled companies to expand their businesses in a tax-efficient manner while making adequate pension provision for the business owners.

A variation on this arrangement is the 'sale and lease back' of existing company premises, under which the trustees would acquire the company's property on an arm's length basis at market value with the company entering into a commercial lease and paying rent to the directors' pension scheme for its continuing occupancy of the premises.

When SIPPs initially came on the scene they were often used in a similar fashion, i.e. to buy premises. Partners in dental and medical practices 'pooled' their existing pensions to acquire surgeries. Some other types of professional practice similarly aggregated their pensions to buy office premises. But unlike SSAS schemes, SIPPs are not allowed to buy existing property owned by the partners and indeed no transactions of any sort are permitted with 'connected persons'. This restricted their use to acquiring new or additional premises and tended to limit their popularity for that reason.

Like SSASs the new plans were allowed to borrow to assist in buying property. The maximum borrowing limit is now 50 per cent of the net assets of the plan (i.e. after taking account of any existing borrowing). Loans are normally secured over the premises and lenders will generally apply their normal lending criteria. One key difference is that in the case of SIPPs the asset is normally owned by a central trustee company rather than by the plan members as individual trustees. Great care is therefore taken by the scheme trustee over matters where any potential liability might arise, for example contaminated land.

A quite separate market for the early SIPP plans which developed was designed to allow investment directly into stocks and shares via stockbrokers. These 'stockbroker managed' SIPPs gained significant popularity among well-heeled professionals who were used to managing their own investment affairs.

Income drawdown

After a period of steadily rising popularity, SIPPs really began to take off in the latter half of the 1990s, following the introduction of 'income drawdown' under the Finance Act 1995 as an alternative to buying an annuity at retirement. Until the introduction of drawdown, individual 'pension pots' had to be converted into annuities at retirement.

Part of the fund could, of course, be withdrawn as a tax-free lump sum, although the option to phase both the tax-free cash and annuities over a period of years had already been available under what were known as 'phased retirement plans'.

This form of arrangement had become popular as it offered a more flexible retirement income than the traditional lump sum plus annuity combination. The ability to phase pension benefits was a by-product of improved systems capability and that allowed insurance companies (and other pension providers) to 'segment' plans into a large number of identical sub-plans. Typically one plan could be split into 1,000 identical segments, each of which carried its own 25 per cent tax-free cash entitlement, and the balance could them be applied to provide pension income via an annuity.

Tranches of these segments could be activated over a period of years so that the retirement 'income' would be made up of a combination of instalments of tax-free cash and layers of annuity building up on each other. In addition to being more tax-efficient, this added flexibility was particularly helpful to people retiring gradually or continuing to work for a period on a part-time basis. It also allowed the retirees to stagger the purchase of annuities and thereby take advantage of the fluctuations in annuity rates which resulted from changes in economic conditions.

The problem of wildly varying annuity rates was often referred to as the 'annuity lottery' and the government eventually realised that it had become a significant disincentive to saving for retirement. This was what prompted the government, in 1995, to take matters a stage further by introducing income drawdown.

The idea behind income drawdown was really quite simple, and for those who can afford to take a continuing degree of investment risk into retirement it has proved to be extremely popular. Having drawn the tax-free cash entitlement the retiree is permitted, rather than applying the balance of the retirement pot to buy an annuity, to draw down a regular income from the investments within the retirement fund within specified maximum and minimum withdrawal limits.

Part or all of the drawdown fund can be applied to buy an annuity at any time up to age 75, but when that age is reached any residual 'unvested' pension capital has to be applied to purchase an annuity. The objectives of the change in legislation were to improve income flexibility and thereby assist retirees in making lifestyle changes; and to avoid the annuity 'lottery', which had resulted in fluctuations in annuity rates of as much as 30 per cent within a matter of a few years.

Income drawdown is not suitable for individuals of modest means, but those who are not entirely reliant on their pensions (whether because they are receiving ongoing employment or self-employment income or because they enjoy other resources) have found the greater flexibility of drawdown to be particularity attractive.

The other major attraction is that on death the residual fund can be preserved for the member's beneficiaries rather than being kept by the annuity provider. In relation to that part of the drawdown plan already activated into payment ('crystallised') a 35 per cent income tax charge is applied to any lump sum death benefit, while any segments or arrangements that had not yet been activated would be tax free on death. In either case, the lump sum death benefit would generally escape inheritance tax as the distribution of the capital is discretionary and would therefore bypass the member's estate.

Nomination of beneficiaries is dealt with through a letter from the member to the scheme trustee, expressing the member's wishes. This can be updated or replaced at any time and crucially is not binding upon the trustee, otherwise IHT would be due. However, that flexibility can create problems as well, if there is a dispute between family members as to who is entitled to what. In such circumstance the scheme trustee will more often than not take the easy option and pay the capital to the deceased member's estate rather than become entangled in a legal squabble between family members. The lump sum would then become subject to inheritance tax (IHT) as part of the estate.

Increased security is achieved by arranging to have the death benefits held under a special form of discretionary trust, and this can be done at any time during the member's lifetime. In most cases this should be a 'carve out' trust rather than a 'pilot' trust as the latter still relies upon the member's nomination via the 'expression of wishes' letter and may be therefore still subject to dispute. However, care needs to be taken in circumstances where the member is critically ill, as a value may then be attributable to the death resulting in an unwanted chargeable lifetime transfer with retrospective tax consequences. In such cases the pilot trust option might be the more appropriate.

Nevertheless, the risks associated with income drawdown are complex and require a sophisticated ongoing investment strategy with appropriate 'risk management' processes if disaster is to be avoided. The greater investment freedom offered by SIPPs therefore made them the natural vehicle for managing income drawdown arrangements.

Modern SIPP plans are generally administered in conjunction with 'fund supermarkets', whereby the SIPP administrators (sometimes an insurance company but often a specialist SIPP business such as James Hay) provide access on preferential terms to the funds of a wide range of fund management companies.

Drawdown investment advisers will undertake to design portfolios using a variety of investment funds covering different asset classes and selected on a 'best of breed' basis. Fund managers include insurance companies and unit trust companies as well as offshore providers.

Using a combination of different asset classes with sophisticated monitoring techniques enables advisers to meet the income requirements of their clients to their best advantage through varying economic conditions. For example, a drawdown portfolio might typically include a range of 8 or 10 funds spread across sectors such as commercial property, fixed income securities such as government securities (gilts) and corporate bonds, higher yielding equities or growth funds, and might combine UK and overseas markets in an overall investment 'blend' appropriate to the risk profile of the individual client.

Annuities can also be bought selectively at opportune moments along the way, taking advantage of favourable market conditions to gradually increase the amount of guaranteed income through a phased 'trade-off' between risk and security which matches the client's changing progressive needs.

Income drawdown has also brought pensions far more into the sphere of estate planning. Investors fortunate enough to have greater resources than they require to meet their lifetime financial needs can decide, with an eye on estate planning, whether to consume their pension assets or to maintain them in situ. Keeping in mind the old adage about not letting the 'tax tail wag the investment dog', the decision as to which of the alternative sources of income should take greater precedence at what stage of retirement becomes a critical factor in the financial planning process.

Annuities

Key to understanding the dynamic of the planning opportunities is the recognition of the unique qualities inherent in annuities. A lifetime annuity is essentially an insurance policy that protects the annuitant's income against the annuitant's own longevity and, in the case of 'joint life' annuities, that of a surviving spouse or civil partner. Unlike any other type of investment an annuity, by definition, cannot be outlived by the annuitant.

Optionally, annuities can also provide insurance against inflation, if the retiree chooses an 'index-linked' annuity rather than a 'flat rate' annuity. It is also possible to partially insure against inflation by buying an annuity which provides fixed rate increases, e.g. 3 per cent per annum.

Fully index-linked annuities are the most expensive but provide the greatest certainty of achieving the essential income requirements for an uncertain longevity.

Enhanced annuity rates are available where life expectancy is impaired through ill health and specialist annuity providers such as Partnership Assurance and Just Retirement will underwrite the terms based on medical evidence.

The unique characteristics of annuities, particularly the index-linked variety, enable them to play a vital role in the overall estate planning process. Mitigating IHT is best achieved by avoiding the prospective liability rather than pursuing the alternative advocated by some advisers, of insuring against it through life assurance in the form of a 'whole-of-life' policy (which is simply a way of funding the tax liability in advance). Shorter-term policies can be useful as contingency cover.

Nevertheless, avoiding a potential IHT charge on death generally necessitates giving away capital during an investor's lifetime, which might compromise his own long-term financial security. This is why pension planning and estate planning are essentially intertwined.

The risk of financial compromise in later life can be avoided by securing the appropriate amount of income on an index-linked basis which, along with other pension benefits including state pension entitlement, will meet the minimum acceptable needs as agreed with each individual client.

While planning ahead for the ultimate annuity purchase, excess resources can be divested out of the estate on a timely basis. In practice this is unlikely to be a single event and more often than not will be a staged process of lump sum transfers to trust, having exhausted the more obvious planning opportunities and tax exemptions along the way.

Nevertheless putting 'longevity financial planning' into context is no easy task. Financial modelling systems can provide a perspective and framework within which planning decisions become far easier for clients. Certain types of trusts also offer progressive solutions which have an eye to the needs of the client and spouse as well as being designed ultimately to mitigate the effect of tax on the estate.

Under current legislation the pension must be 'secured' by age 75 at the latest. Any tax-free cash remaining must be taken before the member's 75th birthday, otherwise the entitlement is lost. Pensions are in most instances secured by means of an annuity. However, the legislation now permits an alternative, known as an 'alternatively secured pension' (ASP).

Introduced under the 'pensions simplification' changes brought about by the Finance Act 2006, when the tax rules were unified, the ASP option allows annuity purchase to be deferred indefinitely. Any remaining ASP fund on the death of the surviving spouse could in theory be passed into new pension plans for family members (or any other nominees) provided they held a pension account with the same SIPP company, and at the time this seemed an attractive option.

However, the government was concerned to avoid pensions becoming a vehicle for avoiding IHT, and after the legislation came into effect the Treasury made it clear that the sole intention of the ASP was to facilitate the continuance of income drawdown for certain religious groups, such as the Plymouth Brethren, who had principled objections to gaining from the death of others – a feature inherent in lifetime annuities.

The potential for ASPs as a means of passing pension wealth down to future generations was therefore scotched by further legislation in the Finance Act 2007 which resulted in a potential tax liability of up to 82 per cent tax on the remaining fund on the second death. The only exception to this rule is if the fund is left to charity. In all other cases the ASP pot would be subject to various technical tax charges amounting in aggregate to 70 per cent of the fund, and the remaining 30 per cent would still fall to be taxed under IHT provisions at 40 per cent.

The consequence of this change is that an election to carry on in drawdown after 75 is no longer appropriate if the primary objective is wealth preservation, as more would be secured for descendants by buying an annuity with a 10-year guaranteed minimum payment period.

There are still certain circumstances under which deferring the purchase of an annuity after the age of 75 will be appropriate. Clients who are terminally ill are often unlikely to be able to secure adequately enhanced terms from specialist providers in the 'impaired life' annuity market, as the risk to the insurer of the annuitant surviving longer than expected is disproportionately high. Deferring annuity purchase would in these circumstances enable the surviving spouse to secure the pension on a 'single life' basis following the member's death.

The cost of including a pension for a surviving spouse or civil partner in a joint life annuity can also be quite significant when the female life assured is many years younger. Women generally live longer than men, and annuity companies charge more for that reason. Consequently, some clients who can afford to remain in drawdown will do so with a view to maintaining the fund at least until their spouse or partner has reached an age at which the joint life annuity terms are more favourable. They are in effect 'self-insuring' the income for a period beyond 75 as the cost of insuring it through an annuity appears unattractive due to the younger female life.

In considering the pension 'exit strategy' for wealthier clients a key issue is to attempt to strike the optimum balance between the advantages of secured pensions (in the form of annuities or more likely a series of annuities taken at favourable opportunities) and the preservation of the pension capital on premature death, taking account of such factors as state of health and the relative age of the spouse or civil partner.

Holistic financial analysis is essential and the advice needs to be ongoing as the interaction between pension planning and estate planning is likely to be evolving throughout retirement at least up to age 75 and sometimes beyond.

21

Pensions and estate planning: a case study

Richard Shanks

Many successful business owners have accumulated substantial personal assets and have in addition made significant contributions through their businesses into pension schemes such as small self-administered schemes (SSASs) or self-invested personal pensions (SIPPs), thereby extracting money from their businesses' tax-efficiently.

The pension accumulation process might have been straightforward, but the de-cumulation phase, of extracting value tax-efficiently from the pension scheme, can often be more complicated. Sometimes this is due to the difficulty in co-ordinating the various inputs of advice; it is not uncommon for a client to have one adviser for their personal assets (usually a financial adviser), one for the business (often an accountant) and another for the pension scheme (either a financial adviser or a pension administrator).

As shown in the following case study, it is much more satisfactory if a holistic view can be adopted which takes into account personal, business and pension assets and the interaction of income tax, capital gains tax (CGT) and inheritance tax (IHT).

> ### CASE STUDY
>
> The client concerned runs a successful business and has significant personal assets and pension assets within an SSAS worth another £2m. The client has just celebrated his 50th birthday and has been advised by the pension scheme adviser to take advantage of the option which is available to members of individual money purchase schemes over the age of 50, of extracting the available tax-free cash from the scheme and commencing the withdrawal of income from the scheme investments under what is known as an 'unsecured pension' (USP).
>
> The client has no intention at present of retiring from or selling the business and does not need any more capital or income. The SSAS's only assets are properties, with a small amount of borrowing outstanding, and the client does not

want to have to sell any of the properties at this stage. The instruction is to provide overall tax planning which takes account of IHT considerations.

In discussion with the client, two main options are considered:

(1) to commence USP immediately, as proposed by the pension scheme adviser; or
(2) to defer taking any pension benefits, possibly until nearer the age of 75, when USP must cease and members must either purchase an annuity or convert to the tax-disadvantaged version of USP known as 'alternatively secured pension' (ASP), at which time the client would need to review his situation again.

The main potential advantages of option (1) would be:

• that this could permit a greater sum to be extracted from the pension scheme over the lifetime of the client, assuming normal life expectancy; and
• that the client would not be caught by the increase in the minimum age for taking pension benefits, which will rise from 50 to 55 as from 6 April 2010.

The main potential disadvantages of this course of action would be:

• that there would be an immediate increase in the value of the client's estate potentially subject to IHT due to the inclusion of the 25 per cent tax-free cash from the pension; in addition, if the client subsequently died after crystallising benefits from the pension fund, there would be at least a 35 per cent tax charge on any residual fund passed on as a lump sum;
• if the client's intention to maximise the amount of cash that could be extracted from the pension scheme, this might necessitate the sale of the property within the SSAS or require significant borrowing, which might not be acceptable to the client. In addition, in this situation a reasonably aggressive investment strategy would be required, which might not be compatible with the client's attitude to investment risk.

The main potential advantage of the second main option, namely that of deferring pension benefits until nearer the age of 75 and then reviewing the situation, would be:

• that this would allow the client to deliberately deplete his personal assets before depleting the pension assets, and thereby reducing the potential IHT liability.

The client's business is eligible for business property relief and therefore could be passed on to the client's beneficiaries on death without any IHT liability. In addition, if the client died prior to the age of 75 before having crystallised benefits from the SSAS, the whole of the fund could also potentially pass to the estate free of IHT and other tax charges. However, the latter benefit might be dependent on the client making a nomination to the SSAS provider to allow the fund to pass to a suitable trust vehicle on death.

Therefore, the client could aim to achieve a significant erosion of those assets which are subject to IHT by the time he intends to take benefits from the pension scheme, in the knowledge that he has access to a significant tax-free cash sum and a source of income from the pension for future needs. Of course, the same logic applies should the client intend to sell the business at some time in the future, although at that time he would have swapped IHT-efficient assets for assets which would form part of his taxable estate and would therefore need to consider further IHT planning in advance of any sale.

The other advantage of the deferral option is that the pension fund has the potential for tax-efficient growth. There is no income tax liability on any rental income received on property held within the SSAS and no tax on other income or gains within the fund (except for unrecoverable tax such as that on dividend income from UK equities).

The main potential disadvantage of the deferral option is that if the client were to die prematurely, he might personally have derived little or no financial benefit from the pension fund. However, this is not of great concern to the client in question, because he has no immediate need for additional capital or income himself and is comfortable in the knowledge that any residual fund would benefit his spouse and/or dependants.

It is therefore important that clients should be made aware of all of the options available to them before deciding whether to crystallise their pension funds by taking pension benefits in the form of annuities (lifetime, investment-backed, short-term or variable or guaranteed annuities), USP or (for those aged 75 or over) ASP; and they should be advised of the main potential advantages and disadvantages of each course of action.

The advice to this client also took account of his capital and income requirements, income and expenditure, tax position and state of health and whether any of these factors were likely to change in the future. The first priority had to be to ensure that the client had sufficient capital and income for the rest of his life.

Calculations were made on the basis of certain assumptions regarding life expectancy, tax position, potential investment growth and annuity rates, which showed the client the financial effect of taking either of the two courses of action outlined above. The objective was to establish how the client could extract the maximum overall value from his pension, personal and business assets, in a manner that was as tax-efficient as possible for the purposes of income tax, CGT and IHT. The assumptions made were realistic, but it was emphasised to the client that relatively small changes to these assumptions would result in rather different outcomes.

The level of income likely to be available under the alternative scenarios was calculated and consideration was given to the consequences of the client entering ASP at age 75, or purchasing a lifetime annuity at that time. These calculations showed that there could potentially be considerable financial benefit for this particular client to defer taking any pension benefits until at least age 75. This also allowed him, in accordance with his intentions, to defer selling the property within the SSAS until market conditions became more favourable and to minimise his IHT liability in the event of his dying unexpectedly.

The final adjustment to the financial plan was to arrange for the rental income to build up within the pension fund rather than be used to expedite the repayment of the outstanding mortgage debt, so that if the client did need any funds in the form of tax-free cash, these would be available.

A different course of action might be appropriate for clients in different circumstances, for example those who are selling or winding down a business and need a replacement income. In such a case, taking pension benefits as early as possible could allow the client to draw and gift the tax-free cash and/or other personal assets (either directly to beneficiaries or into trusts) as part of their overall IHT planning, secure in the knowledge that sufficient income will be available from the pension scheme to last for the rest of their lives.

With any business, it is also important to consider succession planning in the event of the unexpected death or permanent incapacity of one of the owners or key members of staff, ensuring that sufficient financial provision is in place for such an event by way of protection plans such as Shareholder and/or Keyperson Insurance.

In summary, there are many different courses of action available to clients in this situation and it depends very much on their own particular circumstances, priorities and objectives as to which is the most appropriate. It is therefore of paramount importance that they receive tailored, holistic advice regarding their overall situation rather than looking at a single area in isolation. It is also vital that the plan should be reviewed on a regular basis to take into account any changes.

22

Financial planning for the redundant executive

Richard Clark

There is never a good time to be made redundant and whilst redundancies will occur in all stages of the economic cycle they are often most publicised and more commonplace during periods of economic slowdown or full-blown recessions. Redundancies can be an unwanted consequence of many things including the introduction of new technology, cost-cutting exercises and the wind-up of a company or organisation and, whilst it is important to regularly review financial affairs, this becomes even more pertinent if redundancy is likely to occur or, worse still, has just occurred.

Financial planning is generally more of an art than an exact science as every individual financial plan will require something slightly different depending on the required objectives or goals. That said, there are some fundamental issues that should be considered at regular intervals. It could be argued that these issues require more urgent consideration when a major change in situation or lifestyle occurs. This may occur not only on redundancy but also with the arrival of children, divorce, receiving an inheritance or any other material change to an individual's or a couple's circumstances.

Issues that may be particularly relevant to an executive who has been, or may anticipate being, made redundant may include some if not all of the following.

Protection

Protection is generally thought to mean making adequate provision for your nearest and dearest should you either die or become unable to work through illness or incapacity. To some, life assurance can seem a relatively uninspiring part of any financial plan. It is, however, one of the key areas to be addressed. Consider a 'breadwinner' with a spouse and, let us say, two young children. It is important that provision is made such that if the breadwinner dies or suffers a critical illness, the rest of the family will be secure and not fall on hard times. This is clearly an important part of any plan and should be considered as one of the first priorities.

Existing cover

Upon being notified of any redundancy, an individual should review all existing policies they may have to establish whether there are any redundancy benefits. Some policies include a clause that will come into effect in the event of redundancy. For example, some loan agreements include a redundancy option such that the liability may be met during times of unemployment, or a payment holiday may be offered without penalty. Similarly, certain mortgage protection policies will include a redundancy clause. Clearly, therefore, identifying any benefits payable under existing policies in the event of redundancy should be seen as a priority.

Lost cover

Once any benefits under existing policies are identified and an appropriate course of action is taken, the individual should also identify what cover, if any, is in place as a direct result of their former employment. Often remuneration packages under the terms of employment will include an element of protection. This could be, for example, a death-in-service benefit which is essentially life cover which would pay out on the death of an employee. The benefit is usually linked to the employer pension scheme and expressed as a multiple of salary.

Other insurances such as private medical insurance (PMI), permanent health insurance (PHI, often referred to as income protection) and, in addition, some other health related benefits may also be provided as part of a remuneration package by an employer so it is recommended that the individual finding themselves in the redundancy situation is clear about what benefits will be lost following termination of their employment.

Replacement cover

Once a review of any existing cover and any lost cover has been completed, as referred to above, any shortfalls in protection should be identified and a view taken as to whether it is necessary to effect replacement cover in the individual's own name. Clearly this will depend on many factors such as the actual need for the cover in the first place and also any associated costs. Affordability may obviously be an issue here, but effecting cover on a short-term basis may offer a temporary solution.

Pensions

Ex-employees are usually able to retain their entitlement to pension benefits, although the form which the benefits take may change substantially.

Members of occupational pensions should be sent a statement showing the deferred annual pension. A transfer value can then be requested as a basis for comparing the relative advantages of remaining in the ex-employer's scheme or transferring the accrued value to another scheme. Members of group stakeholder or personal pension schemes, on the other hand, should be able to maintain these schemes and continue their own contributions.

Many ex-employees are inclined to want to sever all ties with their previous employer, but this may not be wise when it comes to pensions. One option may be to take early retirement, though this is unlikely to be appropriate if the expectation is that new employment will be obtained, since this could result in the pension income suffering tax at a higher rate than might have been applicable after employment had ceased.

State and employer benefits

State benefits, such as Jobseeker's Allowance, may be claimable if individuals satisfy the relevant eligibility criteria. Further information can be obtained from **www.direct.gov.uk**.

Employer benefits can come in all shapes and sizes, including share incentive plans (SIPs), savings related share option schemes (referred to as Save As You Earn or SAYE), enterprise management incentives (EMIs) and company share option plans (CSOPs). They all essentially represent an additional benefit provided to employees by employers usually in the form of company shares.

In a redundancy situation, an individual should review their existing entitlements and also any potential future entitlements with the aim of establishing a value. Once a value has been determined, a decision can be made as to what to do with any existing shares or likely future benefits. Consideration should also be given as to how appropriate it is for the individual to continue to hold the shares in question, given that the company has been required to make employees redundant. It may also be advisable to consider this aspect in terms of risk, for example is it appropriate for the individual to be exposed to the risks associated with holding a single company's shares?

As well as the elements of protection referred to above that may be offered by an employer, there are often other benefits associated with an individual's remuneration package. For example, the position may have attracted the benefit of a company car and, obviously, when the employment ceases this benefit will no longer be available. Other benefits may include pension scheme contributions, childcare vouchers and petrol cards.

Redundancy payments

Individuals with at least two years' continuous service are usually entitled to a statutory redundancy payment. However, executives on substantial salaries with meaningful service could realistically expect to receive considerable sums as part of their redundancy package. If the redundancy payout is less than £30,000, and only consists of a redundancy payment, then the payment should not be subject to taxation.

A decision will be required by the individual to establish how the most value can be extracted from the receipt of this capital. For example, if the individual has debt, consideration should be given as to whether it is most efficient to pay off this debt as far as possible or, alternatively, to use this payment to maintain a lifestyle while new employment is sought. Debt could be in the form of mortgages or car loans. The obvious ideal position is to have no debt and, therefore, part of the individual's plan may be to investigate how debt could best be reorganised or potentially repaid. Whilst, for some individuals, debt associated with mortgages may continue to be affordable and is often thought to be acceptable, debt such as credit cards or unsecured borrowing is often subject to much higher interest charges and therefore it may be most efficient to remove this debt as far as possible. This is particularly true if interest paid attracts no tax relief as will be the case with most personal borrowing. Paying interest on which no tax relief is obtained out of interest which is taxed is not tax efficient. An individual's protection arrangements may also influence this decision, e.g. if mortgage repayments are covered by any insurance.

Taxation

Tax should be borne in mind when considering any financial plan, though it would be unwise to make any financial plan or financial-based decision solely in order to save tax. It is important to be mindful of the old adage not to let the tax tail wag the investment dog. An executive in a redundancy situation may find themselves in a position to be able to recover some of the tax previously paid as their earnings cease.

An often overlooked aspect of financial planning is ensuring that clients make full use of any available allowances. For example, every UK resident has their own personal capital gains tax (CGT) allowance, which amounts to £9,600 of gains in the 2008/09 tax year. Within this allowance, capital gains can be crystallised free of CGT. Given the recent changes to the CGT regime, it could be argued, at least from a tax perspective, that it is more effective to target capital growth as opposed to income. The rationale is that income will be taxed at 40 per cent for a higher rate taxpayer whereas any capital gains will be offset by the annual allowance and then subject to tax at a maximum flat rate of 18 per cent. Similarly, if capital is available, an individual may like to consider making use of their annual inheritance tax allowance in order to fund gifts.

Investment review

It may be that capital becomes available for investment as a result of redundancy, and the executive may, for example, want to generate as much income as possible. However, any decision should be taken as part of a wider financial plan, involving a review of existing investments.

Will review

It is normally recommended that clients review the provisions in their will at least every two years to ensure not only that these accurately reflect their wishes but also that they are as tax-efficient as possible. Redundancy will materially alter an individual's circumstances and is one of the major turning points in life which necessitate a special review.

Precedents

A. Appointment of IFA as authorised third party
B. Terms of Business for referring law firm
C. Text for financial advice leaflet for use by law firm when referring to an unconnected IFA
D. Letter referring a client to an unconnected IFA
E. Letter advising clients of a hived-off IFA business
F. Text for financial advice leaflet for use by law firm when referring clients to an IFA joint venture
G. Letter referring a client to an IFA joint venture
H. Referral instruction to IFA
I. Heads of Terms for Appointed Representative Agreement

Appointment of IFA as authorised third party

From: (*XYZ IFA*)
To: (*ABC Solicitors*)

Dear Sirs

Referral of clients for financial services

This is to confirm the basis of the arrangement whereby we will provide financial advice to such of your clients as you may refer to us.

1. We confirm that we are authorised by the Financial Services Authority and only ever provide whole-of-market advice. We are not tied to any product provider or group of product providers. In order to avoid any conflict with the activities of professional firms which refer clients to us, we conduct only financial services work.

2. We acknowledge that the clients you refer to us are and shall remain your clients for the purposes of all business conducted by you. We will not provide to any referred clients any services which might compete with the services which you provide and will do nothing to discourage such clients from remaining your clients. When invited we will attend introductory meetings with clients at your offices.

3. We will provide client-facing material to enable you to comply with the requirement of the Solicitors' Financial Services (Conduct of Business) Rules 2001 that you should disclose your status to potential clients, by stating, in addition to your name and address:

    *   that your firm is not authorised by the Financial Services Authority
    *   the nature of the regulated activities which you carry on and the fact that they are limited in scope
    *   that your firm is regulated by the Solicitors Regulation Authority
    *   that your complaints and redress mechanisms are provided through the Solicitors Regulation Authority and the Legal Complaints Service.

4. The material which we provide will also enable you to satisfy the requirement of the said Rules that you should provide to your clients a statement that:

The Law Society is a designated professional body for the purposes of the Financial Services and Markets Act 2000 but responsibility for regulation and complaints handling has been separated from the Law Society's representative functions. The Solicitors Regulation Authority is the independent regulatory body of the Law Society and the Legal Complaints Service is the independent complaints handling body of the Law Society.

5. We will provide to you a supply of instruction record forms complying with the said rules, so as to enable you to complete and return a copy of such record in respect of each client you refer to us, showing their name and basic contact details and the terms of your instruction to us. When appropriate we would also appreciate your providing us with proof of the identity of referred clients, obtained for the purpose of complying with the money laundering regulations.

6. We will send to you copies of the letters or reports containing the recommendations which we make to your clients, showing your firm as copy addressee (so as to remind clients of your interest), and will be pleased to discuss these with you as appropriate.

7. We will assist you to comply with the requirements of the Financial Services and Markets Act 2000 relating to financial promotions by formally approving, in our capacity as an FSA-authorised firm, any marketing material which you may use to promote the availability of our services.

8. We will refer to you any needs which we might identify on the part of referred clients for your mainstream professional services.

9. We will be pleased to provide training to your staff in financial services matters and to participate as may be agreed in any client seminars which you may hold.

10. We will notify you immediately in the event of any potential conflict of interest or other occurrence which might affect our ability to continue accepting your instructions.

11. You have agreed not to offer employment to any member of our staff or management and not to do anything which might encourage any such personnel to leave our employment.

12. This arrangement shall be terminable by either party giving to the other not less than three calendar months' notice in writing.

Yours faithfully

(*Director, XYZ IFA*)

Precedent B

Terms of Business for referring law firm

[ABC SOLICITORS]

Regulated by the Solicitors Regulation Authority

(*address of ABC Solicitors*)

TERMS OF BUSINESS FOR FINANCIAL SERVICES

Many of our clients require financial advice on matters relating to investments, pensions, life insurance and mortgages. We are not ourselves authorised by the Financial Services Authority under the Financial Services and Markets Act 2000 to provide such advice, but we are able in certain circumstances to offer a limited range of investment services to clients because we are regulated by the Solicitors Regulation Authority. We can provide these investment services if they are an incidental part of the professional services we have been engaged to provide and we can also refer clients for specialist financial advice to organisations which are authorised by the Financial Services Authority.

We are naturally concerned when referring clients to financial advisers that the advice they receive should be completely independent and not commission-driven, and we therefore insist that the firms we deal with operate a charging policy similar to that to which solicitors are subject, which requires the adviser to account to the client for any commissions received, and lets the client decide whether these should be offset against fees.

The referral procedure involves our providing a written instruction to the financial adviser firm and, subject to our clients' approval, disclosing whatever client information we may hold which is necessary to the provision of appropriate financial advice. If requested, we will also attend an initial meeting. For its part, the financial adviser firm will explain its own Terms of Business, including its remuneration arrangements.

We ask to see a copy of the financial report produced for each client, so that we can ensure that the proposed financial arrangements are compatible with our legal advice. Please note, however, that no responsibility can be accepted by this firm for any advice given by external financial advisers.

Please note that the complaints and redress mechanisms available to our clients are provided through the Solicitors Regulation Authority and the Legal Complaints Service. If your complaint relates to the financial advice you receive, then complaints and redress are via the Financial Services Authority and the Financial Ombudsman Service.

Please also note the following regulatory statement:

The Law Society is a designated professional body for the purposes of the Financial Services and Markets Act 2000 but responsibility for regulation and complaints handling has been separated from the Law Society's representative functions. The Solicitors Regulation Authority is the independent regulatory body of the Law Society and the Legal Complaints Service is the independent complaints handling body of the Law Society.

Text for financial advice leaflet for use by law firm when referring clients to an unconnected IFA

Professional financial advice

Fundamental to the Solicitors' Code of Conduct are the principles that solicitors' advice must be independent and that they must put the interests of their clients first.

These principles have a special application in relation to financial services, because most financial advisers are not wholly independent. They only get paid when they sell a product; and in many cases they are only able to sell the products of a limited number of providers.

When our clients require financial advice, we work only with professional financial advisers, who account to their clients for any commissions received and possess technical skills which complement our own. By working closely with these advisers we are able to ensure that clients' legal and financial needs are met seamlessly.

SOLICITORS
INDEPENDENT
FINANCIAL ADVICE

(REVERSE)

Solicitors and financial services

Clients are advised in accordance with the Solicitors' Financial Services (Conduct of Business) Rules 2001 as follows:

- We are not authorised by the Financial Services Authority
- The financial services business which we carry on is limited in scope and we refer clients requiring financial advice to a firm of independent financial advisers
- We are regulated by the Solicitors Regulation Authority

- The complaints and redress mechanisms available to our clients are provided through the Solicitors Regulation Authority and the Legal Complaints Service.

The Law Society is a designated professional body for the purposes of the Financial Services and Markets Act 2000 but responsibility for regulation and complaints handling has been separated from the Law Society's representative functions. The Solicitors Regulation Authority is the independent regulatory body of the Law Society and the Legal Complaints Service is the independent complaints handling body of the Law Society.

(name and address of law firm)

Regulated by the Solicitors Regulation Authority

Letter referring a client to an unconnected IFA

Dear (*client*)

I am writing to confirm our discussion, in which I suggested that you should seek financial advice from (*XYZ IFA*), a firm of independent advisers with whom we have worked on previous occasions and who are completely free from the influence of product providers. As mentioned, the type of advice you require can only be provided by firms which are authorised by the Financial Services Authority whereas we, as solicitors, are regulated by the Solicitors Regulation Authority.

I enclose a copy of the form of referral instruction which we completed during our meeting and which I am now sending also to Mr [. . .] of (*XYZ IFA*).

Also enclosed is a copy of (*XYZ IFA's*) corporate leaflet, and I would mention that we have insisted for the protection of our clients that they operate a charging policy similar to our own, which requires the adviser to account to the client for any commissions received, and lets the client decide whether these should be offset against fees.

With your approval, (*XYZ IFA*) will copy us in on whatever recommendations they may make to you, so as to enable us to let you know if these have any legal implications.

Please note that (*XYZ IFA*) is regulated by the Financial Services Authority and its clients enjoy the benefit of the Financial Services Compensation Scheme, whereas the complaints and redress mechanisms available to our own clients are provided through the Solicitors Regulation Authority and the Legal Complaints Service.

Yours etc

For ABC Solicitors

Letter advising clients of a hived-off IFA business

Dear (*client*)

Investment and Financial Planning

(*ABC Solicitors*) have long been responsive to our clients' need for high quality financial advice, having offered this service in-house for over a decade. Indeed, our Investment and Financial Planning department has been so successful that it can now stand on its own feet, and we have reached agreement with the Head of the Department, Mr [. . .], for him to establish a separate company, outside this firm, of which he will be the Managing Director, but in which my partners and I will retain a financial interest.

The new company will provide financial services not only to clients who have until now been served from within (*ABC Solicitors*) but also to the clients of other professional firms in the area. The new firm, (*H-O IFA*), will operate from premises at [. . .]

As has been the case with our in-house financial services department, (*H-O IFA*) will be regulated by the Financial Services Authority, so you can be reassured that the same high regulatory standards will continue to apply. However, because the new company will not be a law firm its clients will not be entitled to the statutory protections available to clients of a lawyer regulated by the Solicitors Regulation Authority. Instead, they will enjoy the protection of the Financial Services Compensation Scheme.

We are conscious that many clients have established close relations with Mr [. . .] and we wish to make the transition to the new arrangements as smooth as possible. We would therefore appreciate your signing and returning the enclosed duplicate copy of this letter in the stamped addressed envelope also enclosed, to indicate your agreement to our transferring your financial services files to (*H-O IFA*).

(*H-O IFA*) will be sending us copies of their advice letters and reports, which will enable us to offer legal advice as may be required.

I enclose an introductory letter and corporate leaflet from (*H-O IFA*) and will be pleased to hear from you if you wish to discuss any aspect of the new arrangements. Please note that (*ABC Solicitors*) will continue to be responsible for any queries or concerns you might have about financial services business which has been conducted in the past.

Yours sincerely

Senior Partner
(*ABC Solicitors*)

Countersigned to confirm agreement to the transfer of financial services files to (*H-O IFA*):

....
Client

Text for financial advice leaflet for use by law firm when referring clients to an IFA joint venture

Professional financial advice

In order to ensure that our clients have access when required to financial advice of a professional quality which is free from the influence of the providers of financial products, we have established an associated company, (*ABC Financial Planning Limited*).

Please note:

- The partners in (*ABC Solicitors*) have a financial interest in (*ABC Financial Planning*).
- (*ABC Financial Planning*) is not regulated by the Solicitors Regulation Authority, so the statutory protections attaching to clients of a lawyer are not available to clients of that business.
- (*ABC Financial Planning*) is authorised and regulated by the Financial Services Authority and its clients enjoy the protection of the Financial Services Compensation Scheme.
- The complaints and redress mechanisms available to clients of (*ABC Solicitors*) are provided through the Solicitors Regulation Authority and the Legal Complaints Service.

ABC Solicitors
Regulated by the Solicitors Regulation Authority
(*address of ABC Solicitors*)

Any Place, Anytown, ZZ1 2AA
Phone: 00000 000000 Fax: 00000 000000
e-mail: firstname.secondname@abc.co,.uk
Web site : www.abc.co.uk

(REVERSE)

Some of the matters on which (*ABC Financial Planning*) may be able to help:

- Personal financial planning
- Investment of personal and trust funds
- Tax and investment planning for personal injury awards
- Pension planning for individuals and businesses
- Financial solutions for estate planning
- Pensions and divorce and collaborative divorce
- Equity release and long-term care
- Financial protection for businesses and owners
- Advice to executives who have lost their jobs

(name and address of associated IFA firm)

Authorised and regulated by the Financial Services Authority

Letter referring a client to an IFA joint venture

Dear (*client*)

The work we have been doing for you in relation to [. . .] requires advice which can only be provided by firms which are authorised and regulated by the Financial Services Authority – which this firm is not. We would therefore suggest that you might consider seeking advice from our associated firm of financial advisers, (*JV IFA*), which does possess the necessary authorisation.

The fact that partners in (*ABC Solicitors*) have a shareholding in (*JV IFA*) assists us in ensuring that the advice which our clients receive is subject to the same requirements as our own advice as solicitors – i.e. that the interests of clients are placed above other considerations and that the advice is completely independent. We have insisted that (*JV IFA*) operates a charging policy similar to that to which solicitors are subject, and which requires the adviser to account to the client for any commissions received and lets the client decide whether these should be offset against fees.

When (*JV IFA*) acts for our clients it copies us in on its recommendations and this enables us to ensure that its advice is compatible with our own legal advice. It also enables us to maintain a more comprehensive overview of clients' affairs generally.

Please note that we, as solicitors, are regulated by the Solicitors Regulation Authority and the complaints and redress mechanisms available to our clients are provided through the Solicitors Regulation Authority and the Legal Complaints Service. Clients of financial advisers such as (*JV IFA*) are regulated by the Financial Services Authority and enjoy the benefit of the Financial Services Compensation Scheme; but they are not entitled to the statutory protections available to clients of a lawyer regulated by the SRA.

A copy of (*JV IFA's*) introductory leaflet is enclosed and, as agreed, we are sending a copy of this letter to Mr [. . .]. of (*JV IFA*) together with a copy of the instruction sheet which we completed at our meeting, so that he can contact you to arrange a meeting.

Finally, I would mention that we are not confined to working with (*JV IFA*), and if on reflection you would prefer to receive financial advice from another firm we will be pleased to advise Mr [. . .] of this and to liaise with the other firm instead – subject of course to being satisfied as to its professional credentials.

Yours etc

For ABC Solicitors

Referral instruction to IFA

CONTACT DETAILS

To: (*XYX IFA*)

From: (*solicitor firm*) . . . .

Fee-earner . . . .

Office: . . . .

Name of client: . . . .

Phone: . . . .

Address of client: . . . .

. . . .

For trust clients, name of principal contact . . . .

INSTRUCTION TO ADVISE

Category of client: ☐ Private ☐ Trust ☐ Corporate

Client's apparent need: ☐ Investment ☐ Pensions ☐ Retirement
☐ Protection ☐ Mortgage
☐ Pension transfer ☐ Other

Scope of advice required: ☐ Comprehensive ☐ Focused
☐ Execution-only

COMMENT

MONEY LAUNDERING Proof of our client's identity is attached:

Yes ☐   No ☐

DATA PROTECTION Our client has agreed to our disclosing relevant information to you ☐

MEETING

☐ Please contact our client to arrange a meeting

☐ We confirm having arranged a meeting at . . . .
on . . . .

Dated . . . .

Precedent I

Heads of Terms for Appointed Representative Agreement

1. Agreement to be between (i) IFA firm (XYZ) and (ii) joint venture between XYZ IFA and ABC Solicitors (JV).

2. XYZ IFA to appoint JV as its Appointed Representative for the purposes of regulation by the Financial Services Authority (FSA).

3. JV to be restricted to conducting activity requiring the same permissions as are possessed by XYZ.

4. XYZ, as principals, to provide professional indemnity insurance cover for JV by including JV as a named person in its own FSA-compliant policy

5. JV to conform with the compliance procedures laid down by XYZ, including compliance audits; to co-operate fully with XYZ and the FSA; and to give XYZ and the FSA access to its files and premises.

6. XYZ to acknowledge JV's proprietorship of its clientele.

7. JV to give XYZ's auditors the same rights of access as they have to XYZ.

8. JV to conduct regulated activity exclusively through the agency of XYZ and as its Appointed Representative and not to represent other market counterparties.

9. JV to produce for XYZ monthly reports of the business which it conducts.

10. In consideration of XYZ providing regulatory, compliance and business support services, JV to pay XYZ . . . . [% of its monthly income] [£. . . . per month].

11. JV to undertake not to disclose to anyone or use for its own or another's benefit any confidential information which might come into its possession about XYZ or its business which JV might acquire during the period of its appointment as Appointed Representative of XYZ.

12. XYZ to be entitled to terminate the Agreement forthwith, without any payment, compensation or damages if it should have reasonable grounds for believing that JV has failed to satisfy the FSA's requirements

for authorisation, whether by reason of issues affecting its solvency, fitness and propriety or otherwise.

13. Either party to be permitted to terminate the agreement on giving . . . . . . months' notice and upon termination JV to deliver to XYZ all compliance documentation, files and other records belonging to XYZ which may be in its possession.

14. On termination, XYZ to ensure that JV is informed that it will no longer be an exempt person for the purpose of the Financial Services and Markets Act 2000; that outstanding regulated activities and obligations to clients are properly completed and fulfilled; and, where appropriate, that clients are informed of any relevant changes.

15. The Agreement to be governed by the laws of England and Wales and JV to submit to the exclusive jurisdiction of the courts of England and Wales.

Index